QUEST

JOURNEY TO THE
CENTRE OF YOUR SOUL

DENISE LINN

WITH

MEADOW LINN

RIDER
LONDON • SYDNEY • AUCKLAND • JOHANNESBURG

First published in 1997

1 3 5 7 9 10 8 6 4 2

Published in 1997 by Rider,
an imprint of Ebury Press, Random House,
20 Vauxhall Bridge Road, London SW1V 2SA

Random House Australia (Pty) Limited
20 Alfred Street, Milsons Point, Sydney,
New South Wales 2061, Australia

Random House New Zealand Limited
18 Poland Road, Glenfield,
Auckland 10, New Zealand

Random House South Africa (Pty) Limited
Endulini, 5A Jubilee Road, Parktown 2193, South Africa

Random House UK Limited Reg. No. 954009

Extract on page 4 reprinted with the permission of Simon & Schuster from *Lame
Deer: Seeker of Visions* by John Fire/Lame Deer and Richard Erdoes. Copyright ©
1972 by John Fire/Lame Deer and Richard Erdoes.

Papers used by Rider Books are natural, recyclable products made from wood grown
in sustainable forests.

Typeset by SX Composing DTP, Rayleigh, Essex
Printed by Mackays of Chatham plc, Chatham, Kent

A CIP catalogue record for this book is available from the British Library

ISBN 0-7126-7292-3

About the Author

Denise Linn's personal journey began as a result of a near-death experience at the age of seventeen. Her life-changing experiences and remarkable recovery set her on a spiritual quest that led her to study the healing traditions of many cultures, including those of her Cherokee ancestors. Her quest took her to a Hawaiian kahuna (shaman), Morna Simeona; Reiki Master Hawayo Takata; the Aborigines in the Australian bush and the Zulus in Bophuthatswana. She was also adopted into a New Zealand Maori tribe. In addition, Denise lived in a Zen Buddhist monastery for over two years.

Denise is an international lecturer, healer and originator of Interior Alignment©, and she holds regular seminars on five continents including one Vision Quest a year. She has authored six self-help books and appears on television and radio programmes throughout the world.

Meadow Linn, Denise's teenage daughter, wrote chapter six of this book and has participated in six Quests. She is a qualified emergency medical technician and is currently in her first year at Williams College in the United States.

By the same author

Sacred Space (1995)
Signposts (1996)

Contents

I dedicate this book to David, who has made all my Quests so enjoyable.

D.L.

I dedicate this book to all those individuals who have been a part of my solo experiences.

M.L.

Acknowledgements

I am thankful to the people who have participated in Vision Quests with me over the years. They have taught me, healed me, and showed me new ways of teaching and living. Without them this book would never have been possible. I also wish to thank every person who recounted their experiences specifically for this book. Because of the large number of people who responded to my request for personal stories, I am not able to acknowledge them all individually here, but my gratitude for their contributions is immeasurable. Each letter enriched my understanding and helped me along in the creative process.

I thank the individuals who have worked with me to make my Quest seminars a success over the years. Especially Lynette Orman and Ellie Baker. These remarkable women have brought wisdom and grace to each Quest. Also, much gratitude to Patti Nugent, Billie Daniels-Braham, Pauline Howfield and Christopher Koller, for their assistance with Vision Quests through the years.

I am immensely grateful to my editor, Judith Kendra, and to Heather Fortner, Mervi Jakonen and Claire Brown for helping this book come to fruition. In addition, I would also like to thank the following people: Deirdre Ahern, Babbette Brown, Lorian Brooks, Marika Burton, Antonia Chavasse, Tony Drew, Lynne Franks, Lili Galer, Steve Heliczer, Matthew Manning, Lele Nacson, Caroline Reynolds, John Rhodes, Maree Thomas, Paul Wigfield, Stuart Wilde and Graham Wilson, for their love and support.

I especially thank my husband David for his continued kindness and compassion. And a very special thank you to our daughter, Meadow Linn, who truly inspired the creation of this book.

A depth of gratitude, as well, goes to my Cherokee ancestors for guidance given during my Quests.

D.L.

A heartfelt thanks to my parents, Denise and David. To my mom who took me on my first Quest at thirteen and gave me the opportunity to write about teenage solos, and to my papa who read my drafts and always told me it was good, no matter how much work it still needed, I'm thankful.

I would like to thank:

- Everyone at the Mountain School for the best experience of my life. I especially thank the director, Anne Stephens, who inspired me to go there, and Kathy Hooke and Holly Williams, who spent many weeks preparing me for my lengthy solo.
- Christine Capone, Abigail Chatfield, Allison Cohen, Sarah Levin, Justin Monroe, Ben Pomeroy, Jessica Taverna and Gwyn Wells who sent me descriptions of their solo experiences.
- The Lakeside Wilderness Program that first took me into the Back Country.
- And finally, Desert Gold. May Coyote Stories live on!

M.L.

Preface

In ancient cultures throughout the world, Quests were used as doorways to enter spiritual realms. Quests could take the form of a retreat into nature, a vision quest or a pilgrimage and, through these extraordinary inner journeys, sacred visions revealed personal direction and life purpose. Traditionally Western culture has had no equivalent rite of passage. We could only imagine how those ancestral people accessed the mystery and wonder that exist at the core of life. However, with the resurgence of interest in spiritual beliefs that are closely interrelated with nature, many people have yearned to return to their spiritual roots. They have felt the call of the Quest.

Over the years, people from eighteen nations have come to the Vision Quest seminars that I have led in various locations around the world. The experience has been immensely rewarding and fulfilling. When participants arrive for a Quest, I hear the same heartfelt concerns time and again: 'Who am I?' 'What is my purpose?' 'How can I live a life that matters?' 'What can I do to heal my relationships?' 'How can I get closer to Spirit?' 'How can I be happy?' Each person comes wanting to find a sacred space within themselves that is real and honest and true.

As the Quest seekers retreat into nature in solitude, shifts of consciousness begin to occur. Old memories come to the surface to be resolved. Fear is confronted. A sense of purpose emerges. In the heightened state of awareness that a Quest elicits, archetypal images can appear. A tree becomes a sage. A cloud becomes an angel. A power song is received. A voice speaks out of the darkness. The unexplained and mysterious occur. Understanding of self deepens and often remarkable transformations take place.

The magic of watching someone confront their fears or take the first steps towards the accomplishment of lifelong dreams has been one of the most fulfilling aspects of my work. Letters received from participants years after their Quests have confirmed that the results are long-lasting and far-reaching. It is the satisfaction I have gained from these observations that made me want to share the Vision Quest experience with a wider audience.

To gather anecdotes for this book, a written request was sent to a number of people who had participated in my Quests. The responses at first came in at the rate of a trickle which rapidly turned into a deluge as letters poured in from many different countries. I was amazed and delighted by both the number and the intensity of the responses I received.

Reading the letters was a very gratifying experience. A consistent theme was the lasting value and impact that the Quest had on life over the years. Many of the letters that were full of glowing adjectives ('It was completely amazing.' 'It changed my life forever.' 'Absolutely the best thing that I have ever done.') weren't used for the sake of journalistic balance because they were too effusive. Some of the most remarkable stories were not included because I thought they would stretch credibility, yet I personally knew they were true. Many of the most touching letters were not used because of the personal nature of the comments, while others were omitted because of a duplication of themes. Deciding which letters to include was a difficult task because each clearly came from the heart.

A number of quotes refer to the island where I currently lead my Vision Quests. Quest participants stay in tipis during the preparation time on the island, which is surrounded by seals, eagles, otters and whales. Wild deer and raccoons roam through the island's forest. Many of the remarks reflect the beauty of such a special place. To protect the privacy of the island's owners, in this book I have changed the name of the island to Sacred Island. It is a fitting name because the island is considered a sacred place by the local Native Americans.

In crediting the source of each experience, some people asked me to use their full name, some asked that their name be changed, others wanted only their first name used and some asked me to use the spiritual name that came to them on their Quest. I have honoured these requests.

Meadow Marie Linn, my eighteen-year-old daughter and a veteran of six Quests, wrote the chapter about teenagers. In her chapter she included journal entries and parts of letters that were sent to her by her friends from the Mountain School in Vermont who shared a four-day Quest with her. Meadow and I both feel passionately about the value that can be garnered through personal retreat into nature. We feel that through combining ancient wisdom and contemporary techniques you can truly journey to the centre of your soul.

1 *In Quest of a Vision*

On the second night of my Quest, I stretched out and lay back filled with the most indescribable peace. Staring up at the night sky aglow with a trillion stars, I started to feel utterly minute with the cosmos stretched out above. Who is this I? What purpose does it have in the whole scheme of things? What was I about to find out about myself? What answers to questions long sought will I receive? Intoxicated by the immediacy of nature and feeling as insignificant as a grain of sand, I drifted effortlessly into a deep sleep. All I knew for sure was that this Quest, whatever else it may be, felt absolutely right for me in that moment.

Tessa Dace

There is a realm beyond the physical senses. It is a realm of mystery and spirit. It is an infinite and eternal dimension that transcends form and goes beyond time and space. The search for this domain has gripped the hearts of human beings throughout history. From the early biblical prophets who walked alone into the desert to fast and pray for divine revelation to Native Americans setting out into the wilderness to search for a vision, the pursuit of an inner world, beyond everyday physical reality, is one of mankind's oldest traditions. For thousands of years humans have retreated into nature in solitude to find answers to life's questions and to gain spiritual wisdom. Though many of the old ways have been forgotten, there is still a means by which anyone in current times can step through the crack between two worlds and enter mystical dimensions. This retreat, this Quest, is an ancient rite of passage; it is a journey to the centre of your soul.

As we hurtle into the future, the trappings of modern life isolate us from the earth and leave little room for the inward quest. We are losing the ability to listen to the stirrings of our soul. In our urban communities we have lost an immediate connection with nature, which is the most powerful purveyor of visions, signs and messages from the realm of Spirit. We have forgotten how to watch these signs, how to listen to the messages in the winds and how to gain wisdom from the trees. Earning money, keeping up with technological advances and raising a family make it difficult to still the mind and open the heart. Hence, very few people truly understand what forces have motivated their life or have shaped their destiny.

Going on a Quest is a powerful way for contemporary people to reclaim a sense of wonder and connection to the earth. This can take the form of a journey into nature for solitude and introspection which encourages answers to personal questions to rise from within. A process of simplification then occurs where you discover what is truly important in life. You can begin to reach the source of any pain you may have so it can be healed. A Quest can also give you certainty about your future as well as help you develop spiritual depth. It is an act of power that can change your life for ever.

There are many ways to embark upon a Quest in present times. You can trek into the wilderness where spiritual realisations are gained through survival, or go on a pilgrimage to a sacred site. However, a Quest can be as simple as taking an afternoon to sit in stillness in a forest or can be experienced in solitude indoors in a room.

One form of Quest requires sitting in nature for three to four days and nights, calling for a vision, which gives guidance about one's life. In ancient native cultures this tradition, called a Vision Quest, was often used as a rite of passage into adulthood because it was felt the visions received by a young man or woman on their Quest helped determine the role they would play as an adult member of their tribe. Later in life they would continue to use this ritualised retreat whenever they needed to gain help from the Spirit Powers.

For those tribal people the Vision Quest was an extension of a religious experience that was based on the earth they walked on, the sky above them and the beauty of nature that permeated every waking moment. Life was seen as one long, mystical sojourn where the Creator spoke to them through every sunrise and every evening breeze. They knew they were constantly surrounded with messages and signs from the spiritual realms, and the Vision Quest allowed them to be still long enough so that they could listen intently to these messages.

In ancient Native American tradition, a vision seeker usually climbed a mountain or went to a special place in nature. Sometimes his sacred site, or 'dreaming place', was a pit dug into the side of a hill. Usually the seeker sat in the centre of a special circle of stones (a medicine wheel) which created a safe and holy place. Often this place for vision seeking had been used by the family for generations. The length of the Vision Quest varied from tribe to tribe; however, the seeker usually stayed for four days and nights without food (and in some traditions without water). One man named John Lame Deer, who later became a medicine man, describes his Vision Quest, near the turn of the century, when he was a boy named Johnny Fire, as follows:

Here I was, crouched in my vision pit, left alone by myself for the first time in my life. I was sixteen then, still had my boy's name, and let me tell you, I was scared. I was shivering and not only from the cold. The nearest human being was many miles away and four days and nights is a long, long time. Of course when it was all over I would no longer be a boy, but a man . . . Blackness was wrapped around me like a velvet cloth. It seemed to cut me off from the outside world, even from my own body. It made me listen to the voices within me. I thought of my forefathers who had crouched on this hill before me . . . I thought that I could sense their presence . . . Sounds came to me through the darkness: the cries of the wind, the whisper of the trees . . . I felt feathers or a wing touching my back and head . . . I heard a voice that was human . . . A voice said, 'You are sacrificing yourself here to become a medicine man. In time you will be one.' Slowly my fear left me . . . I felt power surge through me like a flood . . . when old man Chest [his uncle] came for me, he told me I was no longer a boy. I was a man now. I was Lame Deer.[1]

A Quest of any kind is a heroic journey. It is a rite of passage that carries you to an inward place of silence and majesty and encourages you to live life more courageously and genuinely. The benefits of a Quest are numerous. A Quest can help you to:

- heal relationship issues
- overcome fears and self-imposed limitations
- heal abuse, grief and anger issues
- gain power and clarity
- find your purpose
- define your life goals
- connect to your higher self
- meet your guides, totems and allies
- find your true name
- connect more deeply to nature
- discover who you are

One of the most profound benefits of a Quest is the discovery of who you are through exploring the patterns in your life. There are consistent patterns in all things. These templates for life have grace, rhythm and symmetry and are a part of the great web of the universe. You can find these patterns in the way branches circle a tree or the wind shifts desert sands, as well as in the changing of the seasons and in the continuous cycle of birth, death and rebirth. They also exist within and throughout your life. In the stillness of a Quest you can examine your life's recurring cycles. Wilma Hartman, a communications consultant from South Africa, wrote to me about how her Vision Quest helped her to discover who she was and to realise the rhythms in her life.

During my Quest I sensed a great awareness of cycles. Cycles of day and night, of the sun, the moon, the sound of the tides, of the whale coming back every morning. I sensed my own rhythm. In one contradiction, things both slowed down and sped up. I was intensely aware of Great Spirit being the rhythmic heart pulsing inside me and in everything around me. Everything being one.

Looking back, my Vision Quest dreams leap at me. They are still extremely vivid. One upon the other, they were like skins of fear being peeled away. My dreams were filled with anxiety, fear of change, fear of being rejected, fear of exploring the unknown. Bit by bit I worked beyond the fear until I knew that the life I had was the one I wanted. It was no longer the boring life, forced upon me by responsibility and sense of duty.

I left the island with heightened perceptiveness, with inner strength and a feeling of being part of a great universe. My arms could reach far and wide. Like cool water being drawn through the centre of a big strong tree. I came back home, unable to give words to what I had experienced.

Sometimes a Quest can act as a catalyst for old issues to surface and heal. Lisa, an advertising executive living in Hong Kong, had a very powerful emotional experience that began a healing process for her regarding childhood sexual abuse issues.

I got really angry about not having any water for most of the second day. I had a leaky water bottle. I stormed off my little hump of grass and stamped back to the lodge thinking that I was going to let everyone know just how unfair this water business was. I ranted at an assistant and she burst into tears. Then I went in to attack you [Denise]. I hated you at that point.

You said at the time that the water incident must hold a learning for me, that the anger which had occurred must have a root in the past. No surprise. Of course you were right. Usually, rather than express my emotions in the form of tears, I would cry inside myself. The result of this was that when I was emotional I wouldn't cry, but I would urinate profusely. I realised that having no water had been set up at some level to bring me face to face with the water issue, or more accurately with the natural expression of my emotions.

I had always been aware of my ability to leave my body in times of pain but did not understand the causes. Though I didn't know it at the time of the Vision Quest, the disconnection with my emotions was brought about largely through early and forgotten sexual and emotional abuse. The Vision Quest was the stimulus for a period of exploration and discovery. It allowed me to come to terms with my emotional fragmentation and the integration of the different parts of me. The Vision Quest started a process by which I have worked through heaps of emotional stuff from my younger years . . . rapes and attempted rapes. As a result of this work, one year later I weighed 135 pounds (at the time of the Quest I was around 200 pounds). The insights and way of viewing the universe which I gained have become increasingly integrated into my daily life.

Many people find that a Vision Quest helps them to overcome fear. Julie Robertson told me how the Quest helped her confront fear. She had a difficult time finding the right spot for her Quest. 'Suddenly I stumbled across a little clearing. It was about nine feet around, in a circle of trees, the perfect size for a medicine wheel.' However, once she sat in her circle she began to feel afraid. As late afternoon shadows lengthened with the approach of evening she began to feel even more frightened. She heard many unexplainable sounds in the surrounding woods which 'froze' her 'with terror'. She told me that she was so scared that she felt like she was in a 'waking nightmare'. She said:

As I stared in tired misery at a clump of nearby trees, I felt I was hallucinating. Then the pattern of a mottled feather appeared in the trees. I closed my eyes, reopened them and the feather was still there. Slowly the face of a tawny owl formed over it. I realised that this was a message from Great Spirit that the owl was my guide . . . At this point, I thought of everyone I'd wronged, apologised to them and mentally hugged them. Then I thought of those who'd wronged me and I forgave them. Tears flowed as I experienced total forgiveness of my mother. The wind whispered through the trees, 'You have done well,' and then the trees all swayed gently above me, as if looking down and nodding in agreement . . . And so the process continues which sprang from my Vision Quest. That was a time I shall remember for ever.

Julie's fear was a catalyst for healing and forgiveness.

Sometimes a Vision Quest can carry you into mystic and wondrous realms. This occurred for Krystel Nicol, a young woman with a gentle mien. She arrived for the Vision Quest without a clear direction but found that her Quest opened her to something precious and magic inside herself.

I didn't really know why I came to the Vision Quest, I just felt impelled. I spent most of the time on the island before the Quest trying to come to terms with just being Me . . . the negative Me, the jealous Me, the angry Me, the petty Me, the selfish Me . . . and the frightened Me. The first night of the Vision Quest as I lay down to go to sleep, I felt very frightened of the dark . . . I was so scared that I even began to tremble as I lay in my sleeping bag. Then I began hearing the delicate sounds of bells ringing . . . followed by the soft muffled sound of a gong. I then heard voices coming closer. My fear receded when I heard the voices. As I strained to hear what they were saying I was amazed to hear the voices whispering my name. As I listened more intently the voices became more distinct. I heard them say, 'Don't be afraid. You are safe. We are here watching over you.' The next thing I remember it was morning and deer were eating near the lake not far from my Vision Quest circle.

Later that day at sunset, I heard breaking sticks behind me. I slowly turned around to see a beautiful softly dappled doe standing on the moss-covered forest floor not far from my circle. She blinked. I closed my eyes and silently told her not to be afraid. When I opened them she was still standing and watching me. Very slowly, very calmly she walked closer. Hesitating for just a moment she stepped into my circle and gently brought her face next to mine. I could smell her. I could feel her warm breath on my cheek. I looked directly into her eyes and she let me see her spirit, and I let her into my heart. For a second it felt like our spirits were one, and I knew her totally and she knew me. She showed me how to open my heart, she opened a pathway for the real me to start to grow and for the first time in my life I felt complete!

A Vision Quest can allow you to experience everyday life in a new and vibrant way. Janna Bristow, dental technician, found power in the silence of the night that enriched her day-to-day life.

On the second night I had quite a rough time. I had tapped into all sorts of shadow lands and found myself feeling immensely small and lonely, cold and very hungry. I have never felt so exposed and so tremendously alone. Time stood still and the night seemed to stretch on for ever. I was scared but couldn't understand what really frightened me. The darkness sought me out and exposed me. I sensed being watched, watched by the trees, the rocks, the sky and all the creatures I could not see. The silence was excruciating. I can imagine how some people feel they are losing their sanity when there is just no sound. As I lay there in darkness, unable to move or to distract my mind, I began to engage with other levels of consciousness. I had only once before experienced this, and it was long ago in the desert. I began to connect with the beauty of the silence. It makes me tearful just telling of it, I never want to lose it. Now I can be in the midst of everyday hectic life and I am able to tune in to my inner self, knowing that the great depth of silence is not lost. After a few hours, scenes of incredible beauty . . . mountains, rolling hills, lush green valleys, deep blue lakes and powerful waterfalls, filled my vision. I had entered an altered state of consciousness. It was incredibly soothing and comforting to be able to connect to the spirit world with such ease. I never thought it possible. I then fell asleep for a short while just before dawn.

Some people think that on a Quest one's purpose can only be discovered through struggle and strife. Although the recognition of purpose can come through sustained effort, it can also come as a gentle recognition that you *are* living your purpose, an awareness that everything you have done in your life is meant to be. However, until you have this realisation, it seems that life is without purpose. But life isn't always a mystery to solve; it is more a reality to experience. Graham Walkinshaw, a crisis counsellor from Scotland, talked about his Quest and his realisation.

My Quest was not spectacular. I was hoping for some dramatic vision or visitation. I had positioned my medicine circle near to the shore as I knew that Orca whales swam in the waters around the island. Their presence was one of the reasons for my coming to the island to do the Quest. My scientific, left-brained mentality, which I have always struggled with, wanted some physical encounter, like a message from an Orca, to prove the existence of the visionary world. I suppose that I only partially acknowledged this to myself as I never really expected this kind of thing to happen to me.

In the end I sat quietly in the same space for two days just being.

Thinking about this now, the simplicity of what I did is quite surprising. I sat on one part of the planet for a couple of days and . . . was! I spent a long time watching the ants. A sea otter leaped out of the water, scurried around in the undergrowth then returned silently to the sea. A deer walked right past me, an arm's length away, eating the green grass and moving on without the slightest glance in my direction. Many birds came and went, seemingly oblivious to my existence as I just sat and watched.

It wasn't until I came to write this that I began to appreciate fully the lesson of quietly sitting in one place for a while. I am so used to the hurry and noise of the world that I had forgotten to be simply sitting. I suppose my scientific, left-brained self can't believe that the answer is so simple. Just be!!!

Visions can come in many ways and calling for a vision can be a lifelong process. However, there is power in setting time aside in your life for a Quest. I suggest that your personal Quest consists of six parts.

1. Purpose

The first step entails defining the purpose of your retreat. What is your reason for going on a Quest? Is there an area of your life that needs healing? Do you need to step beyond fears that are immobilising your life? Do you need to seek a new direction in life? Do you need some time just to be still, without having to do anything? These are all valid reasons to embark on a Quest. Where your intention goes, your energy flows, and as you define the purpose of your Quest the universe will propel you in the direction of your intention.

2. Preparation

What kind of Quest are you going to do? How long are you going to Quest for? What location are you going to use? Are you going to use a preparatory programme (see Chapter 2)? Have you dealt with all obligations and cleared the time for your Quest? These are all questions that should be addressed before you go on a Quest.

3. Leaving the World Behind

On a Vision Quest you leave the comfort of the boundaries of your environment and venture out beyond what is safe and secure. When one is always in comfortable surroundings, decisions and experiences are often based on repetitive preconditioned responses. These responses are predicated by one's environment, friends and family. When you take the risk of stepping out of the normal boundary of your everyday experiences, then a fresh new way of seeing yourself and the world around you can evolve. This can be done ideally by going into nature. However, as urban life consistently makes demands on our time and resources, a Quest can also occur in a sheltered environment such as a tent or even a building. It is important that you are in an environment where you do not need to do anything and there are no external distractions such as the phone or visitors so you can truly 'leave the world behind'.

4. Life Evaluation

Who are you? What are you? Often we do things to give ourselves the impression that we exist; how do you know that you exist? What really gives meaning to your life? What are your priorities? Are you satisfied with your career and your relationships? Every act creates its own consequences. What are the consequences of your acts in life? Are you happy with the way your life is going? It is during this time that you can evaluate your personal history and face your fears and your death. This is the time to observe repeating negative patterns in your life and to step beyond limiting definitions of self. This is the time to realise that you are *not* your: past history, culture, society, religion, economic level, race, heritage, family, sex, body, or even your feelings and emotions. It is during this time that you can explore who you truly are. When you take the time to examine your past, it prepares you for your future.

5. Being Open for a Vision

The next step is to let go and be completely open to Spirit. Quieting the mind is important because only when you are empty can you be filled. In the stillness you can 'be' in present time, observe the signs in your surrounding environment and listen to the whispers of the universe. This is the time of symbolic death and rebirth into a new way of being in the world. Learn how to live a life that matters. Your vision helps shape your destiny and those who find their destiny find happiness.

6. Returning Home

Endings are as important as beginnings. Give yourself time to re-enter slowly back into your life and to integrate your experience. When you cross the threshold back into the ordinary world, you may be reluctant to return. Overpowering reluctance may be a form of self-indulgence. You have taken a sacred inner journey, and now you are returning to the people to give something of what you have gained from your experiences to each individual you meet and to the world at large. This is the power of the Quest.

If you decide specifically to go on a Vision Quest, it is best to work with someone who has led these experiences before. However, in modern life it is not always possible to have a shaman or a guide as you seek your signs and visions. You can therefore create a modified Vision Quest for yourself. This book gives you that information. Chief Crazy Horse said in 1850: 'A very good vision is needed for life, and the man who has it must follow it – as the eagle seeks the deepest blue of the sky.' It's important to take time off from your life in order to renew and restore yourself, to balance with all things. A Vision Quest may be the singular most significant thing that you do in your life.

2 Preparing for your Quest

Your Quest starts the moment you make the choice to go. This decision is a heroic step, a commitment to discover and embrace who you are. Your commitment is giving your word to the universe and to your self that you will embark on this sacred journey, and there is power in that. Once you have made the choice, remarkably, it may seem as if life conspires to prepare you for your Quest. Sometimes old issues and personal blockages begin to surface for release during your retreat. Sometimes opportunities, almost magically, present themselves to ease your inward journey.

Forces will have been set in motion beyond the reckoning of the senses. Sequences of events from the corners of the world will draw gradually together, and miracles of coincidence will bring the inevitable to pass . . .

Joseph Campbell[1]

After you have made a covenant with yourself to go on a Quest, decide what kind to go on. There are many different sorts to suit your personality and lifestyle. You may decide to go on an organised guided Vision Quest, go on your own or with friends, choose from a number of 'alternative' Quests, or go on a pilgrimage.

A Guided Quest

There are organisations and individuals which arrange Quests. Some are primarily focused on the Vision Quest and

some simply include a Vision Quest as part of their programme. (See the Appendix for a listing of programmes.) If
you choose to go on an organised Quest it is very important
to do some research into the programme and leaders. Some
are aligned with Native American traditions, while others
have more emphasis on personal development. Some are
aimed at a particular topic, such as a Vision Quest for
women to help overcome emotional blockages as a result of
sexual abuse. Some Quests are designed to be physically
strenuous and some are less intense. One kind of Quest is
not intrinsically better than another; the best Quest is the
one that is best for you.

Ask the organisation to give you the names of some previous participants so you can talk to them about their
experience, and their opinion of the leaders and organisation. Don't be afraid to ask questions. The more confident
you are about the programme you have chosen, the better
prepared you will be for your Quest.

When you are looking for someone to be a teacher or
guide for your Vision Quest choose a person who:

- radiates compassion and kindness
- has a good reputation
- is flexible in teaching style
- has a confident presence
- knows how to listen
- accepts mistakes in self and others
- isn't afraid to show emotions
- has a good sense of humour
- laughs at themselves
- makes everyone feel valuable

- has a playful side
- is direct and truthful
- shows respect for the environment
- includes members of any race or culture.

It is worth choosing carefully with whom you are going to do your Vision Quest. However, in a deeper sense, there are no wrong teachers. The teacher you feel drawn to will be the best teacher for you at that time in your life. Some of my greatest growth has come from teachers who were not perfect people. When I was in my early twenties, I was drawn to a teacher who said he was very spiritual and that he knew great truths. He said if I trained with him, I too might become spiritual. Because I was unwilling to take responsibility for my life, it was simpler to submit to someone else's authority. When I realised that this person wasn't as honourable as he portrayed himself, it was a valuable step in my development. In this way he *was* a perfect teacher for me. If he had been impeccably humble and compassionate, I might still be looking to him for answers and I might have never realised that the answers are inside me. I honour the gift of his teaching: it gave me what I needed at the time.

A Support Group Quest

A Support Group Quest is a retreat that you organise with other people. This has the advantage of offering a mutually supportive environment during your Quest. If you decide to work with a group of people to arrange a Quest, it's a good idea to have several planning meetings. Areas to discuss:

- where will your Quest be held?
- what kind of transportation will be needed?
- what supplies should be taken?
- are you going to do a preparatory programme beforehand? (see p. 48)
- what are your safety contingencies? For example, where are the closest hospital and emergency services to your Quest site?

When choosing an area in nature, pick a place where you are not likely to be disturbed by others. Make sure that family and friends know exactly where your group will be and what your timetable is. In addition, if you are on national park or forest land, give the same information to the rangers so that in the event of a natural disaster, such as a flash flood, they will know where to contact you.

If your group Quest will be outdoors, plan to have at least one person serve as a guardian who doesn't do the Quest but who sets up a base camp and conducts safety checks twice a day. (In my Quests I have approximately one guardian for every five or six people.) In addition to the individual supplies listed later in this chapter, the guardian should have emergency supplies including a first-aid kit, extra blankets, camping knife, extra water, food, additional dry clothing in case of bad weather and a means of communication such as a mobile phone or a VHF radio. The guardian can eat and do normal outdoor activities as long as their primary focus is the safety and well-being of the Questers.

A prearranged signal, such as a coloured flag by the Quest site, should be organised so that if a Quester needs anything, such as a plaster, it can be easily obtained. A note left by the flag can give all the necessary information to the guardian. When I check on Vision Quest sites I usually get an okay hand signal from the participants. No words are spoken. Often people sleep for long periods of time on their Quest. If the guardian checks and the participant is sleeping they should continue to check periodically during the day. Usually the Quester is simply taking a long nap, but just in case they have fallen ill, it's a good idea to continue to check and ask them if they are all right.

Be sure to take a whistle with you on your Quest. If you need immediate assistance, a loud blast will bring other Quest members and/or the guardian to your assistance at once. Respect the importance of other people's Quests and do not disturb them for any reason other than an emergency. Before the Quest begins, sit in your Vision Quest site and blow the whistles to make sure that others can hear you.

At the completion many groups celebrate with a meal and share experiences.

Independent Quest

An independent Quest is done without a group. However, do not go into the wilderness for a solo Quest without a guardian. Taking someone with you can be a good experience for both people. I know a couple who went into the wilderness for a Quest. The husband put up a tent and made a camp site while his wife created her sacred circle for a three-day Quest. The husband, who was an artist, painted the mountain scenery for the duration of his wife's retreat. The wife said that although she couldn't see her husband's tent, she felt safe knowing that he was close. They both found the experience very rewarding.

Alternative Quests

Although the kind of Vision Quest that I focus on in this book is a three-day outdoor retreat, there are many different ways that one can Quest. An alternative Quest can be as simple as having a day of silence. It's important to remember that results occur outside time and space. They can occur as a direct outcome of your intention. If your intention is to transform and heal your life, it will happen no matter what form your Quest takes.

Garden Quest

Not everyone can go into the wilderness for a Quest because of health concerns, time constraints or safety issues. For these individuals, an excellent place for a Quest is in the garden. Though this may seem less majestic than a Quest in the wild, a retreat in one's garden can be as powerful and life-transforming as one on a mountain peak. *When your heart is open and your intention is clear, your vision will come, no matter where you are.* The preparation for this type of Quest is the same as if you were doing your retreat in the wilderness, and your sacred circle is created in the same way as described in Chapter 3. However, if your garden doesn't have stones or twigs to make a circle you may need to gather stones beforehand. The equipment you need is essentially the same as for a wilderness Quest, especially if you are doing an extended Quest. However, you will most probably go indoors to use the toilet and to replenish your water supply.

You may want to sleep outdoors in your circle, but if you have health or safety concerns, you can sleep indoors. A garden Quest can last from a few hours to a few days in length.

Indoor Quest

At some of my Quests, for various reasons, several individuals have chosen to do their Quest indoors. In all cases they reported remarkable experiences, which has led me to believe that indoor Quests can be very beneficial. There are advantages to being in nature for your Quest, but in the winter or in bad weather you may choose to be inside. An indoor Quest has the advantage of offering a warm sheltered environment where you can truly focus on your life issues without concern about weather, temperature, poisonous insects or wild animals. It can be profound and moving, particularly if you have taken the time to prepare yourself and the environment.

When preparing for an indoor Quest it's important that the room you use becomes a sacred space. To do this, pick a room where there is as much natural lighting as possible, preferably one with a view of nature but that offers privacy from the outside world. Once you have chosen the room, clean it thoroughly. Wash the windows. Scrub the floors. Clean cobwebs from the ceiling. As you are cleaning, hold the intention that you are creating a sacred place. Clear out as much of the clutter in the room as possible. The more you can clear out of the room, the better. Once the room is clean, you may want to work with the energy in the room by using Space Clearing techniques.[2]

To cleanse the energy in the room, take a small amount

of burning sage in a fireproof bowl and circle the room, using a feather to disperse the smoke to purify the energy. You may then want to take a sprayer filled with water and essential oil to spray the room lightly. A suggested combination of lemon, lime and orange essential oils can help uplift the energy in the room.

When the room feels good to you, bring in objects that represent energy, strength, healing and love. For example, you might want to put a beautiful flower in a vase in the room, bring in a healthy vibrant house plant, or place a faceted lead crystal in the window to make rainbows in the room when the sun shines. You can create your sacred circle with stones or twigs that you have brought in from outdoors or use objects that have special meaning to you. For example, I knew of a young woman who used crystals, feathers and polished stones to create her circle.

Make sure that you have cleared the time, turned off the phone and notified people of your intention so they won't worry about you or disturb your Quest. There is a wondrous power that occurs when you take the time just to sit still in a room within your sacred circle.

Day of Silence

Being silent for a day can be a type of Quest. Simply not talking for a day can allow the internal chatter to become still to the point where you can begin to hear the whisperings of your soul. It may seem a bit contrived at first, but taking a day of silence can turn energy inward. To have a silent day let friends and family know what you are doing so you can gain their support. Turn off the phone, put on the answering machine and no matter how tempting, don't answer the door, don't read your post, don't watch television or listen to the radio or the stereo. Be still. You can walk inside your home. You can take a walk outdoors, particularly if you can be fairly assured you are not going to meet someone who will want to talk to you. You can prepare food. Taking twenty-four hours to be silent can bring profound insights into yourself and your life. Even if you live alone and don't usually talk during the day, the commitment to be silent brings a special energy. Start your day of silence when you wake in the morning until you wake the next day.

If you live with other people and if it's absolutely necessary to communicate, use notes. Susan was married and had three young children under the age of seven. She told me she wanted to do a Vision Quest but didn't see how it was possible with the responsibilities of her family life. I suggested that she have a silent day. She talked to her family and they agreed to be supportive; in fact the kids were excited: 'Mommy is not going to talk all day.' Although a few times the children forgot and addressed her, for the most part they were very supportive. A baby-sitter came to take the children to a park for most of the day and her husband looked after the children in the afternoon and evening. Susan said it was one of the most delicious experiences of her life. She sat in her garden under a large apple tree, sipped fresh mint tea and watched the clouds sailing by. Everything seemed to slow down until whenever she moved she felt as if she were moving through golden honey. She noticed the way the oak tree had been full of gnarls in its youth and then straightened again. She said looking at the oak tree she felt that the 'gnarls' in her life would eventually straighten up again. She lay on the grass and seemed to be aware of the roots of the grasses and plants and the oak tree beneath the surface. She felt an awareness of the myriad activity in the earth; insect activity and even the micro-organisms beneath the surface. It gave her a sense of the living spirit that surrounded their home even though they lived in the city. A day of silence rejuvenated her and connected her to her spiritual roots.

Pilgrimage

A pilgrimage is a type of Quest. Though the form is different from the traditional Vision Quest, often the outcome is the same. Whereas a Vision Quest will allow you to seek answers to soul-searching questions through the inward journey, a pilgrimage can allow you to discover your life's meaning through the outer journey. In some respects a pilgrimage is a mobile Vision Quest. You can call for a vision on your pilgrimage and visions and insights can be received in the same way as on a stationary Quest. A pilgrimage is not just a physical journey through time and space, it is a powerful metaphorical rite of passage that can touch you as deeply as the Vision Quest.

When deciding whether to go on a Vision Quest or a pilgrimage, it's valuable to assess your personal temperament and the reasons for your Quest. Each individual needs to create and express their own inner journey in accordance with their needs and temperament. If you are always on the move and every day is filled with activity and you are consistently directing your energies outward, the stillness and serenity of a Vision Quest might be a balancing influence in your life. However, if your life feels stagnant and you tend to be introverted, then perhaps the pilgrimage is the best kind of Quest for you. Having to deal with new and challenging external situations can catapult you from safe inward landscapes and allow the power and majesty of outer landscapes to transform you at the deepest level.

Where Do You Go on Your Pilgrimage?
The location you choose is very important. Is there somewhere that you have always felt drawn to? Is there a special place that fills you with excitement and wonder every time you hear about it? Here are some of the types of location that you might consider.

1. A sacred site
There are places on earth that are thought to be charged with a spiritual power such as Stonehenge, Machu Picchu or Lourdes. Some are widely known and some are known only to a few seekers. There is a deep current of energy that illuminates these places and a pilgrimage can connect you to the sacred space within you.

2. The location of an early childhood remembrance
A pilgrimage to the location of your childhood can help reclaim lost or abandoned parts of yourself. Sometimes returning to the place of your birth or the place of early childhood memories brings a sense of coming home to yourself. A pilgrimage to the past can also help heal childhood wounds.

3. An ancestor's or relative's grave or ancestral lands
Taking a pilgrimage to a relative or ancestor's grave or to your ancestral lands can be redeeming. When you reclaim a connection with your family roots and your lineage, this can have a sustaining and strengthening effect on your life.

4. Reliving the journey of another
In 1693 the renowned poet Matsuo Basho embarked on an 800-mile journey on foot through Japan's remote mountain regions writing poetry the entire way. The pilgrims who follow his pathway today feel that his clarity and spirit imbued the land and created an energy that can still be felt today. I'm not suggesting you follow Basho's route, but when you follow in the footsteps of another it is valuable to attempt to see and feel as they did.

5. Feeling compelled without a particular end goal
Sometimes your destination becomes compelling, even if you don't have any conscious reason for going. If you feel a deep inner compulsion to journey to a particular sacred site or location, listen to your heart and trust that there is a higher wisdom motivating you. Sometimes the reason will become obvious and sometimes perhaps you will never know, but, nevertheless, it is important to follow the stirrings of your heart.

Your pilgrimage doesn't have to take you to foreign lands across great seas. It can be as simple as journeying to a nearby place of power or beauty. The earth is covered with numerous places of power. Your pilgrimage can be to the top of a nearby mountain, or to an ancient grove of trees or to a cliff overlooking a nearby sea. It is not the length of time you spend or the location you choose, it is truly your intention that allows your pilgrimage to be viable and powerful.

Steps of a Pilgrimage

The steps of a pilgrimage are similar to the steps of a Vision Quest. Both involve a journey that separates one from ordinary life. Both involve an encounter with the sacred and then a homecoming. Here are some important steps to consider on your pilgrimage.

1. Intention

The first step in designing your pilgrimage is to clarify your intention. Why do you want to go on a pilgrimage? What specific results do you want? Take time to clarify for yourself exactly what your purpose is. This is similar to the first step you take before a Vision Quest. When you clarify your purpose, then everything that occurs on your journey is laden with meaning and value and every experience propels you towards your goal.

2. Preparation

The preparation is both physical and emotional. Take time to plan for your physical needs. For example, if you are driving, is your car in good repair? If you are walking, do you need maps? If you are going overseas, is your passport in order? Whether your pilgrimage only takes a few hours in the afternoon, or is a month-long sojourn, it is important to be prepared. Take a journal and use it. The experiences that may seem so mundane at the time may seem meaningful upon later perusal.

3. Separation from ordinary life

Both on a Vision Quest and on a pilgrimage you leave the comfort of the boundaries of your environment and venture out beyond what is safe and secure. Be willing to take a risk and operate without knowing the exact outcome of every decision. When one is always in comfortable surroundings, decisions and experiences are often based on repetitive pre-conditioned responses, dictated by one's environment, friends and family. When you take the risk of stepping out of the normal parameter of your everyday experiences, then a fresh new way of seeing yourself and the world around you can evolve.

4. The Journey

You can walk or drive on your pilgrimage. You can spend a few hours to a number of months. You can choose a route that is easy or one that is challenging. The amount of time you spend, your method of travel and the difficulty of your pilgrimage are not as important as the intensity of your devotion to your journey. Your decision to go on a pilgrim's journey should not be made lightly. Once your journey begins, every experience you have is valuable and salient to the ultimate outcome. A pilgrimage is an act of power.

5. The Destination

Calling a trip a pilgrimage doesn't always make it one. When you reach your destination it is essential to stay in touch with the meaning of your pilgrimage. Take time to embrace the energy undercurrents of the place. Be open and receptive to the messages that are waiting for you at your destination. You have embarked on a long and perhaps even arduous journey to attain your goal. Ask yourself: 'Why am I here?' 'What messages are here for me?' Call for a vision (see Chapter 5).

6. The Ceremony

In ancient times pilgrimages were accompanied by ritual and ceremony. In present times you can either perform the rituals of the past or you can create your own. When you reach your destination, take time to honour your journey. From a simple act of placing a flower on a shrine, to creating a circle of stones, to offering a prayer, ritual actions affirm and deepen the meaning of your experience.

7. Returning Home

Be as conscientious at the completion of your pilgrimage as you are at its inception, for endings are as important as beginnings. Give yourself time to re-enter slowly back in to your life and to integrate your experience. When you cross the threshold back into the ordinary world you may be reluctant to return; overpowering reluctance may be a form of self-indulgence. You have taken the sacred journey, and now you are returning to give something from your experiences to each individual you meet.

Vision Walks

American philosopher and poet Ralph Waldo Emerson wrote, 'Every object, rightly seen, unlocks a new faculty of the soul.' A simple adaptation of the pilgrimage Quest is to go on a Vision Walk. To go on a Vision Walk simply walk out of your front door (or anywhere) and walk with the intention that valuable insight will be gained during your walk . . . and watch for signs. This is especially powerful when you have a problem or challenge in your life. A Vision Walk can be a short ten-minute walk or can entail a longer hike. Your focused intention and observation of signs sets this kind of walk apart from just an afternoon stroll.[3]

Equipment List for a Vision Quest

If you decide to go into the wilderness for your Quest, you will need to take equipment with you. Packing for this can help you clarify the forms of your Quest through the decisions that you have to make. Will I take this? Do I really need that? This is not unlike the decisions that you will encounter in life. How much do you really want to carry in life? Realise that packing for your trek is an act of power. It is a transformative and empowering process. Do you really want to carry that much equipment? Are you denying your needs out of fear about what others will think? Your loaded backpack can be symbolic of your burdens in life. Notice how you feel about it after it's packed. Do you feel over-burdened or perhaps incomplete? What do the different things that you have decided to bring say about you and your life?

This is an optimal list of items that you might consider bringing on your Quest. You may find that you do not need many of the things on this list. However, it's better to decide consciously beforehand what you want rather than be in the middle of your circle and suddenly realise too late that, with your fair skin, you should have brought a hat or sunscreen lotion.

Backpack

If you are hiking into your location you might want to have a backpack to carry your equipment in. If you have never walked with a backpack before, load it up and practise wearing it ahead of time to check and see how it fits on your body.

Clothing consistent with climate and environment

Know the general climate of the area and within those parameters wear enough clothing so that you can layer for warmer or colder temperatures. If you are in cooler weather bring a warm hat to prevent losing too much body heat. Remember that a climate that is comfortable when you are walking will feel substantially colder if you are just sitting and aren't eating. I have known minimalist individuals who have done their Quest nude, but this takes extreme discretion for reasons of personal privacy and in so far as the climate may change.

Waterproof jacket

Even if the weather seems fair, it's usually a good idea to have a jacket that can offer some protection from the rain and wind.

Personal items

What you decide to bring on your Quest is individual. Some

people prefer not to take any personal items. However, others bring items such as a toothbrush and toothpaste, dental floss, comb, hand cream, or feminine hygiene products.

Signal flag

If you are doing a Quest with a guardian, then it's valuable to have a signal flag to hang outside your circle to indicate that you need something. If you don't wish to speak, you can leave a note near the flag.

Sleeping bag and mat

Keep in mind the terrain as well as the climate for the type of sleeping bag you use. I personally prefer the old-fashioned type of large, oversized heavy cotton sleeping bags. They are made of a natural fabric and don't make the rustling noise of the synthetic sleeping bags. However, in a moist climate they will absorb moisture and are damp to sleep in. Also they are heavy to carry if you are walking far. Down sleeping bags are good for cold climates and are lightweight to carry. Fibre-filled bags are the best for rainy conditions. Some people like to bring a mat to go underneath their sleeping bag.

Pillow

If you choose to bring a pillow, a foam or polyfill pillow is better than a feather one as they dry quicker if it rains.

Groundsheets and rain tarps

It is a good idea to have a groundsheet to put under your

sleeping bag and a rain tarp to put over you, in case of rain. The tarp should be about eight by ten feet. In addition, pack nylon cording in case you decide to tie up your tarp. A simple shelter can be constructed by tying a tarp by its metal grommets to nearby trees.

Torch

Bring a torch for emergencies. Check the batteries and make sure it is in good working order. A water-resistant torch is best.

Sunscreen and/or a hat

These items are particularly important if you are going to be exposed to the sun to prevent sunburn or sunstroke.

Insect repellent

Beware of taking so many precautions that you completely insulate yourself from nature. Bugs are a part of nature. No matter where you have your Quest, unless you are indoors, there will be bugs. You can spend time groaning about what a nuisance they are, or you can realise that they are all an important part of Spirit's creation. If you decide to bring an insect repellent, try it beforehand to ensure that you are not allergic to it. Make sure that you have knowledge about the insects in the locale that you have chosen. If there are any poisonous spiders or insects in the area, check with local naturalists to find out the best strategy for dealing with them.

Journal and pen/pencil

For some, using a journal can deepen their experience. For

others, the simpler the Quest the better. If you do decide to use a journal, I suggest you start using your journal from the time that you decide to go on a Quest. Also, consider how you want to keep your journal. Is it purely and utterly for you alone, or are you keeping it so that some day others (children, family, friends) can benefit from your experiences? Who are you writing for? Your perceived audience can determine the form and style of your journal.

Toilet paper and small trowel

When you leave your circle to go to the toilet, it is important that you do not harm the environment. Keep more than 200 feet away from a water source. Also, for obvious sanitary and aesthetic reasons, you should bury any human waste, using a small shovel or hand garden trowel.

Paper bag

Any used toilet paper should be put into a paper bag and burned at a later time. Alternatively toilet paper can be put in a zip-lock plastic bag for a hike out. For environmental reasons, do not leave your used toilet paper in nature, even if it is buried.

Large water container and water

In some traditions, it is belived that a Vision Quest must be done with no water. However, I feel it is important that you have enough water on your Quest. The value gained from depriving your body of water does not equal the damage that might be done by depriving your body of enough fluid. Please drink plenty of water on your Quest. I suggest taking a gallon for each day that you are out. *You do not need to suffer to grow spiritually.* A plastic water container with a screw-top lid is a good idea. Sometimes, in the middle of the night, small animals can chew through the water containers. If you are in an area with animals, reinforce the water bottles with insulating tape to prevent this. Do not drink any water from a natural source that has not been treated or filtered.

Food

Traditionally Quests are done without food. Unless you need to eat for medical reasons (for example if you are diabetic or hypoglycaemic) you might try doing your Quest with very little or no food. As a culture, we tend to have many emotional issues surrounding food. Going without food for a few days can allow some of these issues to surface. However, there is no dishonour in taking food on your Quest. If you do so, be very clear that it is your choice, rather than feeling guilty about it. Whether you eat or not doesn't define the value you will gain. Rather, it is the way that you relate emotionally to the food issue that will determine the value gained. Whatever you choose to, honour your choice and commitment. Personal power doesn't come from whether you choose to eat or not eat; the power comes from making a commitment and abiding by your choice with no regrets.

Food taken on your Quest should provide energy, such as fresh and dried fruit rather than chocolate bars and crisps. Also, it should not spoil easily without refrigeration. Nuts or dried meat are a better source of protein than something that might spoil such as tuna sandwiches. Take all the food for your Quest into your sacred circle with you. However, if you are in an area where animals may be attracted to your food, such as bear country, then the guardian may safeguard your food and bring it to you.

Insulating tape

Insulating tape is an optional item, but if you are going to an isolated area it can come in handy in numerous ways. For example, Dan rolled over his glasses in the middle of the night and broke them. A bit of insulating tape temporarily fixed them and they were usable again. Insulating tape can be used to close a hole in a sleeping bag or ground sheet and has any variety of uses.

Check-off list

- Clothing consistent with climate and environment
- Waterproof jacket
- Personal items
- Sleeping bag and mat
- Pillow
- Groundsheet and rain tarp
- Torch
- Sunscreen or hat
- Insect repellent
- Journal and pen
- Toilet paper
- Paper bag
- Large water container
- Water
- Food (if needed)

- Insulating tape
- Backpack
- Whistle
- Nylon cording

Frequently Asked Questions

What exactly do I do on my Quest?

Sit. Stand. Lie down. Sleep. Think. Meditate. Stretch. Pray. Sing. Dance. Open your heart. Be still. Talk to God. Nap. Watch the environment around you. Breathe. Write in your journal. Cry. Laugh. Let go. Forgive. Heal. Love. (For additional suggestions, see Chapter 4.)

What if it rains? Should I stop?

If it rains, stake or tie up your rain tarp. However, if it does rain during your Quest, this is an important part of your experience. Feel the rain. Become the rain. Listen to what the rain has to say to you. One of the most powerful Quests I ever conducted was in the rain. From the moment the Quest started, it rained. And then it rained harder . . . and harder. Some people ranted at the rain with anger and frustration. The rain became a perfect catalyst for unresolved areas within life. One person who was working through victim issues declared to the heavens above, 'Why are you doing this to me? Why me?' Another person who abandoned every major love relationship because she felt restricted said, 'I want to leave. I feel so restricted by this damn rain.' Slowly, as one wet day slipped into another, a realisation dawned for many. The rain wasn't the victimiser or a restriction or an angry god. The rain was just the rain.

I was told repeatedly by the Quest participants afterwards that the results were much more profound *because* of the rain. Everything that happens on your Quest can be a catalyst for change and growth.

What if I don't get any visions? Did I fail?

Some of the most profound life-changing Vision Quests have been seemingly uneventful at the time. Meredith is a good example of this. She said she felt she was just sitting in her circle. She watched the sun come up and watched it leave again. She felt peaceful at times and bored at times, but it seemed like nothing really happened. She was expecting to see signs and have visions and amazing dreams. However, looking back she reported that while, on the surface, nothing seemed to be occurring, something very profound was shifting inside her because her life changed completely in the following year.

A few months after she came home, she realised that she could no longer stay in the computer job she had held for seven years and which she didn't enjoy, so she quit. She then got a volunteer job, which turned into a full-time job, teaching art to children, which she loved. And the best part was that within three months of the Vision Quest she entered into a wonderful relationship. Meredith said this seemed like a miracle because she had been single, without any major relationships, since a disastrous divorce sixteen years previously. She said she thought that she would never be in a loving relationship and now she is with a 'perfect man'. Even though it seemed that very little happened on her Quest, actually amazing things were happening inside her. When you have the *intention* of being on a powerful inner journey during your Vision Quest then no matter what happens, you will reap results. (For additional information see Chapter 5.)

How long should my Vision Quest be?

If you are going on a Quest with a leader usually the length of the Quest is predetermined. However, if you are going on a self-led Quest, I suggest starting with a very short time; even a few hours in stillness alone in nature can be valuable. You should work up to a longer Quest rather than jumping right in. Remember, it isn't the amount of time you spend, but the value you get from the time that is important.

I've decided to do my Quest without food. Is there anything I can do to prepare for this?

Food can play a powerful role in our emotions and often decisions and judgments about ourselves and our life are based around food. Food can represent love. It can represent self-sabotage and it can also be associated with control issues. Eating is also one of the most strenuous routines in life. And often routines can limit our spirit. When you change your eating patterns it can affect other habits, routines and patterns.

As your Quest looms ahead, notice any issues that arise around food. If you are clear that you are going to Quest without food, you might want to practise going without food. Try skipping a meal or two. Notice how you feel emotionally as well as physically. During the week before your Quest I recommend that you begin to change your eating habits. Allow your body to begin to detoxify. Cut down on fried and/or processed food, meat, dairy products or anything that is hard to digest. Eliminate alcohol and drugs (with the exception of prescription drugs). Focus on the intake of fresh fruits, vegetables, brown rice, fish. Cut down on caffeine. Drink lots of water. Get plenty of sleep and in general prepare your body to be as healthy and strong as it can be during your Quest. This preparation stage will increase your sense of focus and readiness for your Quest.

Should I take my mobile phone?

If you take your mobile phone, use it only for an emergency and ignore it otherwise. However, leave everything else mechanical at home, such as radios, CD and tape players, and portable computers.

What about wild animals?

Animals can be a wonderful source of inspiration on a Quest. Some of the most magical experiences on Vision Quests have involved animals.

If you are going on a guided Quest, make sure that the leader knows about the animals in the area and gives you adequate information if any precautions are needed. If you are going on your own, make sure that you and your guardian are well aware of the animals in the area you have chosen and if any precautions are needed. For example, if you choose an area where there are snakes, you should not choose a site that would be next to a snake habitat. Most animals in nature will not attack if unprovoked, but it's always best to be knowledgeable about the terrain of your Quest.

Sophia attended one of my Quests. In the middle of the night she felt a rather large heavy animal walk on top of her. She lay very still as the animal proceeded to turn in a circle to make itself comfortable. It then curled up in a ball and promptly fell sound asleep. Sophia and the other Questers had been informed about the animals in the area, so she realised that the nestled body was a raccoon which, though they can bite, are not usually considered dangerous animals. She said it was quite a wondrous experience having a wild animal sleeping on her all night. Sophia's experience with her furry visitor was a powerful, positive experience because she was equipped with useful information about the animal . . . and she knew that her life was not in danger. It's valuable to learn as much as you can about all the local wildlife for safety purposes. It is also helpful because it connects you more deeply to the surrounding environment.

Can you leave your circle to go to the bathroom?
Definitely leave your circle. Remember to be environmentally prudent with your used paper (see section above).

What about washing yourself?
Usually you don't wash; however, if not washing will distract you from your Quest then you might consider bringing a damp flannel in a zip-lock plastic bag. Some people feel the need to take a toothbrush and toothpaste. If you do this then please take care that you are not putting needless toothpaste into the environment.

What if I feel ill? Should I stop?

If you don't feel well, tune in to your intuition to see what the best course of action is. If you feel that you have a medical condition coming on, have it attended to right away. Don't ignore the physical signals that your body is sending you. However, sometimes you won't feel well because old issues are coming to the surface to be resolved. If this is the case, it's valuable to push through them. Sally was on her Vision Quest when she felt a cold coming on. Her nose became stuffed up and her eyes began to water. She decided that the cold was brought on by underlying emotional issues so she meditated to examine her innermost feelings. Spontaneously, she began to remember long-forgotten incidents from her childhood. A well of grief filled her as she cried for the first time in many years. Although she had a cold on her Quest, she felt that it was an important catalyst for her to resolve childhood traumas.

If you are feeling ill and are the kind of person who toughs out the hard situations in your life, you do *not* need to tough it out. Sometimes an act of power is to be willing to surrender and be easy on yourself. Suffering doesn't always build character; sometimes it's just suffering.

I have a medical condition; can I go on a Vision Quest?

Anyone can go on a Vision Quest provided they have tailored the Quest to their own individual specific needs. If you have a medical condition explain *very clearly* to your physician the nature of your proposed Quest. It's important that you have her or his approval and support. If you are going on a guided Quest make sure that the Quest leader knows the exact nature of your condition and has the phone numbers of your health care providers. In addition, make sure that someone checks on you periodically during each day. If for any reason you feel unwell, it's important that you take care to guard your health, even if this means shortening your Quest.

There is more personal power gained in knowing what your body needs and making decisions based on supporting your body rather than suffering needlessly. If you are doing a Quest without a leader then it is essential that, in addition to your physician's approval, you have a guardian who is within voice distance, can check on you during the day and has the phone numbers of your health providers. Provided that you approach your Quest with forethought and safety in mind there is no reason why you can't have a successful Quest.

Should I continue taking my medication?
Absolutely. Under no circumstances should you stop taking any vital medication. You do not need to suffer to grow.

I'm diabetic. Is it all right to go without food on my Quest?
No. It is *essential* that if you are diabetic (or hypoglycaemic or have any condition that suggests that you take a consistent calorie intake) you *must* take food on your Quest in accordance with the needs of the body. In addition make sure that you have the support of your health provider.

What if I get scared?
One of the purposes of the Vision Quest is to begin to over-

come fear. If a fear comes up, you can use your circle as a safe place to explore and release the fear. However, if you have a paralysing fear, take some steps to safeguard yourself emotionally. For example, if you are terrified of the dark, bring a torch with extra batteries. You may decide not to use it, but you have it as a back-up.

Lena was completely terrified of the dark. She always slept with a light on at night and had never once slept in the dark. For Lena the most terrifying thing in the world was being alone in the dark. It was a fear that paralysed her. We discussed different options before her Quest. She had a torch to use that gave her a sense of comfort and I told her I would continually check on her during the first night. We also talked about guardian angels and how she had an angel that looked over her during the night and day. After it got dark I went to check on her. I was amazed to find her relaxed and smiling . . . *and sitting in the dark*. This was a very dramatic switch from the white-knuckled terror she had experienced prior to beginning her Quest. She said, 'My angel is with me. I feel so safe and protected. I am safe in the dark. I don't need you to come and check on me.' Tuning in to her spiritual protectors, Lena had activated a sense of safety so that she was able to overcome a lifelong fear. She is no longer afraid of the dark.

Here is an exercise you can do if you find yourself feeling afraid on your Quest.

1. *Locate the exact place in your body you are experiencing the fear.* Every emotion has a corresponding physical sensation and location in your body.

2. *Focus your awareness on that part of the body.* Really feel the fear. Usually when we experience fear, we do everything *not* to feel it. What you resist persists, so the harder you try *not* to feel fear, the more it will persist.

3. *Expand the sensation of fear and make it more intense.* Now this might sound completely crazy. Why would anyone who was feeling afraid want to feel more fear? Two things occur when you do this. First, usually when you are afraid, you are a victim of your circumstances and not feeling in control. When you choose to feel fear rather than being the victim of fear, *you* are in control. When you are in control of your fear it will dissipate. Sometimes we will pay money to be afraid. For example, we pay to go on a roller-coaster or go to a scary movie. The difference in the experience is that you have consciously chosen to become afraid so you are not overwhelmed by the fear.

   The second reason for intensifying your fear is so that you can uncover the experiences from the past and inner issues that continue to dictate that emotion. When you continually suppress your fear, you never have the opportunity really to examine and deal with the underlying issues.

4. *Ask yourself these questions.* If your fear had a shape, what shape would it be? If it had a colour, what colour would it be? If it had a texture and a temperature, what would they be? If there was an attitude (irritation, loneliness, melancholy, etc.) associated with this sensation, what would it be? If there was an emotion (fear, anger, sadness, etc.) associated with your fear, what would it be? Continue to ask yourself these questions over and over as you continue to focus awareness on the fear. Do this until you can be the observer of your fear rather than the victim of it.

5. *Notice if you have any past memories associated with your fear*. If a fearful memory comes into your awareness, imagine that you are floating above it and viewing it from a higher perspective. Understand that every experience you have allows you to become a more integrated, compassionate human being, even experiences that you deem as negative at the time. Once you have found a memory associated with the fear, see if there is an earlier similar memory. Keep going back into early similar memories until you find a 'seed' memory so you can resolve it.

A 'seed' memory is an original experience that all the other future similar experiences are based on. For example, if someone is bitten by a dog when they are five years old, this might precipitate a future fear of dogs. Then perhaps, when that child was seven, riding a bike, a dog begins to chase him. Having a fear of dogs, he becomes frightened and falls off the bike. This experience strengthens and magnifies his fear of dogs. Perhaps another time a dog begins to bark and the child becomes startled, trips and falls backwards. Every experience magnifies (and subconsciously justifies) the original fear. Every similar experience is stacked on top of the original experience. To release a fear, going through the stack of fear experiences, one at a time, can help you get to the original fearful experience. When you understand the dynamics of why the fear originated in the first place, often you can heal it. Many people have healed lifelong fears in the sanctity of their Vision Quest.

Another way of dealing with fear is to call upon your guides, totems and spirit guardians for assistance. This often proves to be a very effective way of dealing with fear (see Chapter 5).

Is there anything I can do beforehand to prepare for my Quest?

You might want to consider going through a preparatory period immediately prior to your Quest. Although it is not essential, a process of physical and emotional preparation can have great value. You will have a much more powerful Quest if you have cleared space in your life beforehand. If you are thinking about the bills that need to be paid or the phone calls that you haven't returned, it makes it more difficult to focus on your Quest. In a deeper sense, if you clear space in your life you are symbolically clearing space within yourself. This can contribute to a more profound Vision. There is power in symbolic acts. For example, if you symbolically clear clutter from your home this contributes to clearing clutter out of your energy field. I suggest going on a twenty-eight-day preparation programme (one full moon cycle) which is based on the medicine wheel (see Chapter 3 for information about the medicine wheel). In this programme, each week is dedicated one of the four elemental areas: air, water, fire and earth. Each of these elements represents one of the four quadrants of the medicine wheel and each relates to a different aspect of your life: mental, emotional, spiritual and physical.

You can initiate this programme any time throughout the year. However, when you begin, be aware of the cycle of the moon. It is ideal to start three to five days before the full moon or the new moon. This means that when you complete the preparation period, one month later, you will be Questing during either of these phases. The moon affects the energy of your Quest, so the phase of the moon during your Vision Quest is important. If you want to take some risks in life and dramatically change the course of your life, you might consider doing your Quest during the full moon which is the time of activity and outer expression. If you feel the need to withdraw into yourself and awaken inner dreams and wisdom, then you might consider doing your Quest during the dark of the moon, which is the time of introspection and inner awakening. It is best to embark on your personal Quest immediately after the twenty-eight-day programme so that there is not much time-lag after your preparatory period.

This twenty-eight-day programme can be done on your own or you can form a support group and do the exercises together, meeting once a week to give each other support. In the weekly meeting you can compare notes on personal progress and offer advice, assistance and encouragement. During the meetings a Quest location is decided upon, usually a location where all participants can go together so they can be in close proximity during the Quest for mutual support.

Days 1–7 AIR: Your Mental Self

This week is dedicated to clearing the mental self

Deep within each of us are different aspects of our personality. The mental component is the part that has the capacity to discern, analyse, evaluate and judge. The first seven days are devoted to clearing as many as possible of the cobwebs and unresolved issues that block the mental aspect of self so that you are mentally prepared for your Quest. Air traditionally represents the mental body, so this is also the time to be aware of the air around you and within you. Mental challenges may come your way this week as an opportunity to clear old mental blockages.

For seven days, when you first awake in the morning, focus on the air around you. Take a deep breath and be aware of the physical air around you. Concentrate on the air as it enters your lungs when you inhale and exhale. By doing this you are activating the Spirit of Air that dwells within you and around you.

During the Air Week:

- do things you've been putting off or make a plan for doing them
- organise papers
- answer letters
- make postponed calls
- pay bills or make a planned schedule to pay bills
- organise your house and office space
- clear out the clutter in your home (if you don't love it or use it get rid of it).

Days 8–14 WATER: Your Emotional Self

This week is dedicated to clearing the emotional self

The emotional aspect of self contains intuition, trust, feeling, childhood emotions, innocence and nurturance, and water traditionally represents emotions as well as purification and cleansing. Don't be concerned if emotional issues occur in your life during this week. All is not always as it seems. The issues that occur during this week can spur an awakening of deeper inner issues . . . and it is all a part of a healing process.

For seven days, when you first awake in the morning, focus on the water around you and within you. According to some estimates the human body is three-quarters water. In addition, there is always water in the atmosphere around you. Even in the driest climate there is always some moisture in the air. Imagine that you are aware of the water that is around and in you. When you take a bath or shower be aware of the cleansing and purifying aspect of water. Focus your awareness and attention on the Spirit of Water and continue to do this periodically throughout each day for the entire week. By doing this you are activating the Spirit of Water that dwells within you and around you.

During the Water Week:

- completely clean your house
- clean your office
- clean your car
- spend time evaluating your relationships
- have you been wanting to say something to someone? Now is the time to say it
- explore your dreams
- follow your intuitions.

Days 15–21 FIRE: Your Spiritual Self

This week is dedicated to clearing the spiritual self

Fire is related to the spiritual aspect of self. It is your life force, the spark of life within you, the kundalini energy, the pure white light within, and the holy flame. Fire also represents transformation and change. Any spiritual blockages in your life may come to the surface during this week. This is the week to begin to change old limiting patterns and habits, which can lock you into repeating negative cycles in life. We often react to situations because of pre-conditioned responses based on outmoded ideas about ourselves. Even tiny changes in your routine, such as changing what you have for breakfast, can help you begin to transform your definition of self. Don't be surprised if unexpected events or spiritual insights occur during this week. No matter what form they take, they will contribute to you stepping into an expanded energy within yourself.

Each morning this week, when you first awake, focus on the fire around you and within you. Light is an aspect of fire. If there is any sunlight in your bedroom imagine that you are breathing in its light and power. Focus your awareness on the interplay of light and shadows in your surroundings. Fire dwells within you as your life force, the bio-electrical current that surges through the energy meridians in your body. Be aware of the inner flame within you. Continue to focus on fire in all its aspects periodically throughout each day for the entire week. By doing this you are activating the Spirit of Fire that dwells within you and around you.

During the Fire Week:

- meditate twenty-four minutes a day on your inner light
- listen to those inner voices urging you to branch out in a wholly new direction in your life

- change your routines and your habits
- change your hairstyle
- take a new route to work
- try out a new food you have never had before
- buy that new outfit you thought was just a bit too wild (or elegant, or casual) for you. Wear it!
- make a list of five things that get you all 'fired up' – either angry or inspired – and take constructive action.

Days 22–28 EARTH: Your Physical Self

This week is dedicated to clearing the physical self

All the solid forms around you, including your body, are a part of the physical realm. Ancient peoples understood that everything we see and touch – every stone, every tree, our bodies and bodies of all creatures we encounter – all are connected to the body of Mother Earth. This week is focused on your connection to physical reality. Be aware of the sense of grounding that your relationship to physical objects can give you. You are not separate from the universe. You are related to everything you see, touch, taste, hear and encounter.

Every morning for seven days, when you first awake, focus on the physical nature of your environment. Be aware of the shapes and textures of objects around you. Get a sense of the solid physical nature of your body. Notice how you relate and identify with the physical universe around you. Fully explore all the information brought to you through your bodily senses. Be aware of your time on this planet in the physical plane. By doing this you are activating the Spirit of Earth that dwells within you and around you.

uring the Earth Week:

- notice your relationship to all the physical objects in your home and life. What do they say about you? What do they symbolise for you?
- go for a walk every day. Spend at least twenty minutes in nature in silence. Know that you are a part of everything you see and touch
- attend to your health, e.g. have your medical check-up, dental check-up, etc.
- be conscious of your physical body sensations. Get a massage or do something to contribute to your physical well-being
- go on a cleansing diet. Eat fresh fruit and vegetables; cut back on protein and animal products; drink lots of fluids.

Day 29 Preparation/Travel Day

Days 30–33 VISION QUEST
(See Chapter 4)

3 The Sacred Circle

Your entire Vision Quest is a rite of passage and a ritual. Rituals are important in all cultures past and present. Though they are more often associated with earth-based cultures, rituals are still honoured in Western cultures in rites of passage such as baptism, marriage, graduation and funerals. They mark important transitions in life, serve as a link with past generations, and offer a sense of continuity and security. In a deeper sense, rituals offer a way to express spiritual realities; they are physical enactments of inner spiritual voyages. Ceremony and ritual can allow for a deeper connection between the human and the divine realms.

One method of going on a Quest entails using ritual and ceremony to create a circle out of stones or twigs within which to sit during your retreat. As you dwell within this sacred space, you will be participating in an ancient ceremony that spans generations and cultures. You then become part of a lineage that stretches behind you and unfolds in front of you. When you create your sacred circle not only are you empowering the old ways but you are creating an energy for those who follow after you.

In past times native people honoured the sacred circle and what it represented. The circle was so important that it played a central theme in native ceremonies throughout the world. Many homes were made in the form of a circle. Rituals of purification were done in the circular sweat lodge. When the elders came together in council, it was in a circle so that all were included, each having an equal say. Sacred dance was done in a circle. The circle evoked the feeling of completeness and wholeness; it allowed one to align with the centre of the universe. The circle represented totality; the beginning and the end.

Although the use of a sacred circle during a quest is universal, I have chosen to use the Native American term 'medicine wheel' for the circle you will create on your Quest. To comprehend the medicine wheel, one must first understand the Native American concept of medicine, which is very unlike Western, allopathic medicine. Native American medicine encompasses nature and concerns those things which help you to achieve a greater connection to Spirit. It increases your strength, health and personal power and teaches you how to become more in balance with the world around you.

Your Vision Quest medicine wheel is a physical representation of the sacred circle that encompasses all life. It is an outer manifestation of an inner force. In its deepest sense, the medicine wheel is the pulsating cycle of energy that infuses all matter, animate and inanimate. It is symbolic of the mandala of the universe in which everything created has its appropriate place. It represents life, death and rebirth. It contains the four elements and the four directions. Jacob Boehme, a sixteenth-century mystic, wrote: 'The Being of God is like a wheel, wherein many wheels are made one in another, upwards, downwards, crossways and yet continually turn all of them together. At which indeed, when a man beholds the Wheel, he highly marvels.'

When you enter the medicine wheel on your Quest, you are stepping into a place of prayer. The centre of the medicine wheel is sacred ground; it is a place of peace, calmness and light. It represents a safe place where the Creator dwells. The Hopi Indians have a word, *tuwanasaapi*, which means the place of belonging, the place where you are in your true home, the centring place, or the spiritual axis of the universe. The medicine wheel that you create for your Vision Quest becomes a point where you can pass between the visible and invisible realms. It becomes your centring place, your *tuwanasaapi*. It marks a sacred place of openness, love, unmasking of the true self, sincerity of heart, transformation, giving thanks, and reaching for the stars.

Not only is the medicine wheel a sacred place for your Vision Quest, it is also a circle of protection. In Ancient European tradition, the magi put a circular shield around himself that sealed him from his surroundings. This circle of power protected him and became a place where energy could build. Those early mystics understood the sanctity of the sacred circle. Using ceremony, intent and love, your medicine wheel can be a protected sanctuary where a vortex of spinning energy can build. As the vortex spins, your prayers can ride on this powerful energy and whirl upwards to your higher self and to God. This mystical, twirling energy of light and sound can take off the old and outdated parts of self, while the seed of love inside you is purified.

The Wisdom of the Four Elements and the Four Directions

It is important to comprehend the significance of the medicine wheel that you create for your Quest. Your understanding will empower you. My perception of the sacred circle came from training with many native teachers. In most traditions the wheel is divided into four quadrants. Each of these quadrants represents different qualities, such as the four cardinal directions (east, south, west and north), and the different elements (air, water, fire and earth). Though the meanings vary between tribes and cultures, there is a general consensus concerning the power and value of the medicine wheel. However, each cultural group has its own system for assigning various qualities, colours, elements and totem animals to the cardinal points of the medicine wheel, and these may vary widely between divergent traditions. In my search for understanding, this was disheartening because I was searching for the 'true' medicine wheel.

For several years I searched for the 'right' wheel system. Then one day I realised that if one system was 'right' then the other systems were wrong . . . and this didn't feel good to me. *All* medicine wheel traditions have truth and beauty. The value of the medicine wheel is in the general way that it gives structure to the understanding and honouring of the inner cycles within us.

When I realised that the 'true' medicine wheel was the one that was true to me, I decided to embark on a deep inner journey to find my own wheel. Before I began my inward voyage, I prayed to the Creator and asked for a vision in which I could receive the information that was best for me. My eyes closed; my breathing became deeper and slower. The sounds of the birds at first seemed very loud, then their raucous chirping faded to muffled faint sounds until I was completely shrouded in dark silence. A deep sense of quietness came over me as the following images filled my mind and being.

Suddenly the darkness was pierced by a pinpoint of intense light. I could feel myself being sucked towards that light. As I passed through a vortex-like portal of light, I felt alternate warm and cool shudders surge through me. Below me I could see a circular clearing in a meadow surrounded by mists.

As I floated down, I noticed the meadow was surrounded by tall old trees. I intuitively knew that these tall silent guardians were each radiating loving wisdom and strength, creating a circle of power by their presence. Below me was a large circle of stones. Each stone was smooth and round, like a river-bottom stone smoothed by years of swiftly flowing waters; each seemed to shimmer softly in its own light. As my feet touched the ground, in the centre of the circle, I could feel intense freedom, power and love emanating from the earth. A mist began to form around the circle.

I took a moment to be still. I then faced towards the east and said, 'Spirit of the East, help me understand my way in the world,' and I stepped out of the stone circle into the mists. A soft wind began to swirl around me, shifting and changing. The light breeze became a whirling wind. I could feel all the forms of air spiralling around and even through me: cyclones, jet streams, zephyrs, tornadoes and finally the stillness of a calm. Then, like a whisper, a delicate shimmer of energy rippled through the air as the wings of an eagle soared overhead. I felt the Air Spirits 'talking' to me. I gained the understanding that the element of air represents the intellect, mental clarity, focus, creativity and inspiration. Taking a breath, I felt the Spirit of Air fill me. I realised that I was not separate from air as it dwells within and around me. Giving thanks to the Spirit of the East, I stepped back into the circle of stones.

Facing towards the south I again stepped out of the circle into the mists. 'Spirit of South, hear me. Show me my way.' Through the mists I saw overlapping images of gentle rains, waterfalls, mountain streams, gentle undulating seas, fierce ocean waves, torrential rains, soft mists and fog, snow and ice – all forms of Spirit of Water. The Water Spirit spoke to me of emotions and childhood innocence and sacred dreams. I felt the water that flowed through my veins connect me to my feelings, my childlike wonder, and to trust and humility. I realised that I was not separate from the water that flows through and around me. Giving thanks to the Spirit of the South, I stepped back into the circle of stones.

I turned to face the west and again stepped into the mists calling for the Spirit of the West. Blazing, bright light illuminated the mists. Images of fire, from candlelight to campfires to forest fires to the setting sun filled my consciousness. The Spirit of Fire spoke to me of transformation and spiritual renewal. I was told that fire represents the alchemy that occurs when you release the old and embrace the new, as form changes and is transformed through fire. Fire changes old patterns and old habits; it is purification and renewal. The spark of life in every cell in my body is symbolised by fire. I recognised that I was not separate from the infinite sun and the life force within all things. Giving thanks to the Spirit of the West, I stepped into the circle again.

I faced north. Even before I entered into the mists, I could feel the cold chill from the realm of the north fill me. As I stepped forward I could feel the immense power of the earth beneath my feet. Her many forms appeared and disappeared in the mists: her mountains, her valleys, her rolling hills and deep canyons and vast plains. The Spirit of the Earth spoke of the physical realm of the world and the ancient wisdom that dwells in her depths. She spoke of balance, consolidation and introspection.

With reverence I thanked the Spirit of the North and stepped into the centre of the wheel. The centre is the point beyond the four directions and the four elements. It is the resting place of the Creator. It is the formless form, the place where beginnings and endings merge. In the centre I felt a deep sense of tranquillity. I found my medicine wheel and was at peace.

As I listened to the whispers of Spirit in the four directions, I began to understand the cycles within my life, my own journey around the medicine wheel of life. I recognised that each part of the wheel symbolised a different aspect of myself and my life. In psychological terms, each quadrant of the medicine wheel represents a different aspect of my personality: the mental, emotional, physical and spiritual aspects of my life. The beauty of the wheel philosophy is that the centre of the circle is the place where all these aspects come together and are integrated; where all the parts of self are in harmony. The centre of the circle is the dwelling place of the Creator where the forces of the universe merge into one.

My inner journey allowed me to comprehend the spirit of sacred circle. In further explorations, I discovered cycles within cycles of the medicine wheel. There is no end. The capacity for human development through the wheel is infinite. The sacred circle turns for ever, and the journey never ends. It is a healing tool that can be used to soothe the soul by aligning with the elements and moulding together the fragmented parts of self.

My wheel gives me joy and stability. I have included the information I gained as a starting point for understanding the power and beauty of the sacred wheel that you will create during your Quest. You may find that these meanings work for you, or you may want to use a sacred circle from a culture with which you feel an alignment, or you may want to discover your own personal medicine wheel.

Spirit of the East

Symbolically the beginning of the medicine wheel is in the east. The east is the home of new beginnings. It is the home of the spring, the dawning of the day and the waxing of the new moon. New life. New birth. Seeds are planted. New sprouts pushing through the soil. Eggs in nests wait to hatch. Babies are born. The colour associated with the east is yellow and yellow-green, because this is the colour of plants when they first sprout in the spring filled with a potent life force. The element associated with the east is air which symbolises the mental aspects of self. The key word is inspiration. The animal spirit keepers are eagle, representing the masculine aspect of the east, and owl, which represents the feminine. The eagle's realm is the day, which symbolises the outgoing, projecting, yang forces of the universe. The owl's realm is the night, which symbolises the inward, receptive, yin forces. In the creativity cycle, the east is the place of activation of an idea.

Spirit of the South

Moving around the sacred circle in a clockwise direction, from the east you journey to the south. The south is the home of summer, the midday sun and the full moon. Corn is high. Days are warm. It is the time of fullness and expansion. As the east represents a time of birth, so the south is associated with growth and the time of childhood. The element associated with the south is water, which symbolises the emotional aspects of self. The colour of the south is blue, for it symbolises the deep blue of the sea and great waters. The animal spirit keepers are frog and dolphin, the masculine and feminine aspects of south. The frog waits patiently for his prey and then projects his tongue forward with focus and precision. This represents the yang masculine energy of linear projection and direction. The dolphin has a panoramic awareness of her environment, which is more yin and embodies the female principle of the universe. The key word of the south is intuition. In the creativity cycle, the south is the place where you nurture an idea.

Spirit of the West

In the cycle of life, the west is the realm of autumn, the setting sun and the waning moon. Crops are harvested. Leaves are falling from the trees. In the human cycle, the west is associated with teenage and young adult years as these are the years of change and maturation, discovery, transformation and experimentation. Fire is the element associated with the west, representing the spiritual aspect of life. The key word for the west is transformation. The colour associated with the west is the bright red of the setting sun. The animal spirit keepers of the west are the phoenix and the snake. The phoenix (which can be likened to the thunder-bird of the Native Americans), is the masculine aspect which embodies the transforming nature of fire. The snake, the feminine aspect, also represents transformation as the snake changes when its skin is shed. Snake (lizard in some native cultures) is the keeper of the dream time. In Hindu philos-ophy the snake represents the kundalini life force fires that dwell at the base of the spine which has the power to trans-form body and soul. In the creativity cycle, after you activate an idea in the east and nurture it in the south, you then experiment with it in the west. To put an idea into form, you need to see what works and what doesn't work. In order to do this, you must experiment with an idea, watch-ing it change and go through various transformations.

Spirit of the North

As you complete the circle, you arrive in the north. In the cycle of life, the north is the realm of winter, the darkest night, and the dark of the moon. It is also completion and consolidation. In the human cycle the north is associated with the achievement of maturity, the accomplishments of the middle years of life, and the transition to old age, the elders, grandmothers and grandfathers. The north is also the realm of death and rebirth. The colours of the north are the stark white and black of winter. The medicine power of the north is wisdom and introspection. There is a powerful inner knowing that comes from being connected to the earth.

The element that dwells in the north of the medicine

wheel is earth, which symbolises the physical aspects of self. Earth energy is grounding, allowing you to stand your ground in times of adversity. Earth is not only the surface of the ground which you can see, but also the rocks and stones and boulders underneath. Earth includes those things that have roots firmly embedded in it, such as trees and plants. In the cycle of creativity, after you activate an idea in the east, nurture it in the south, experiment in the west, you consolidate it in the north. The north is also the place of ancient wisdom. The key word for the north is introspection. The animal spirits in the north are bear and turtle. Both hibernate in the winter and go into the darkness. The bear, a dramatic symbol in myth and lore because of its power and speed (up to forty miles per hour for short distances), is the masculine aspect of the Earth. The turtle is the feminine aspect. In the Far East, the turtle's shell is a symbol of heaven and the underside is a symbol of the earth; thus the turtle represented blessings from heaven and earth. In Native American lore the turtle was associated with the lunar cycle, feminine principles and was a symbol of Mother Earth.

Below are the different aspects of the Medicine Wheel:

	East	South	West	North
Quality	mental	emotional	spiritual	physical
Element	air	water	fire	earth
Season	spring	summer	autumn	winter
Sun	dawn	noon	sunset	midnight
Moon	waxing moon	full moon	waning moon	new moon
Colour	yellow	blue	red	black/white

Human	birth	childhood	young adult	elder
Creativity	activation	nurturance	experimentation	consolidation
Key Word	inspiration	intuition	transformation	introspection
Animals	eagle/owl	frog/dolphin	phoenix/snake	bear/turtle

There are fundamental energy differences between the northern and southern hemispheres that will affect your medicine wheel. However, it is easy to adopt the above medicine wheel to the southern hemisphere. Energy moves clockwise in the northern hemisphere and counter-clockwise in the southern hemisphere; therefore it is appropriate to travel the wheel in a counter-clockwise manner in the southern hemisphere. In the northern hemisphere the north is home of the winter, cold and darkness; however in the southern hemisphere the south is the home of winter. Therefore the qualities of the north and south in the medicine wheel are reversed in the southern hemisphere.

The Location for your Circle

It's important to decide the general location for the circle for your Quest ahead of time. Traditionally a person on a Vision Quest would look for a spot that was elevated and had a view. However, the best place for your Vision Quest is the place that feels best to you. Each kind of terrain offers its own special qualities. For example, if you decide to have your Vision Quest in a valley or a crevice this can offer an energy that can feel womblike, comforting and protected, and can contribute to focusing your attention inward.

An elevated place can have the advantage of allowing you to gain a wider perspective of your life. When you are able

THE MEDICINE WHEEL

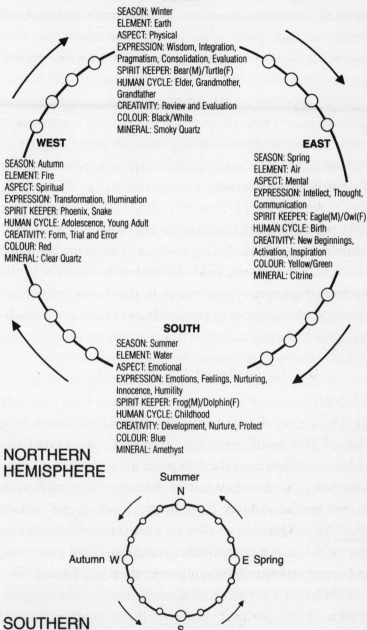

NORTH

SEASON: Winter
ELEMENT: Earth
ASPECT: Physical
EXPRESSION: Wisdom, Integration,
Pragmatism, Consolidation, Evaluation
SPIRIT KEEPER: Bear(M)/Turtle(F)
HUMAN CYCLE: Elder, Grandmother,
Grandfather
CREATIVITY: Review and Evaluation
COLOUR: Black/White
MINERAL: Smoky Quartz

WEST

SEASON: Autumn
ELEMENT: Fire
ASPECT: Spiritual
EXPRESSION: Transformation, Illumination
SPIRIT KEEPER: Phoenix, Snake
HUMAN CYCLE: Adolescence, Young Adult
CREATIVITY: Form, Trial and Error
COLOUR: Red
MINERAL: Clear Quartz

EAST

SEASON: Spring
ELEMENT: Air
ASPECT: Mental
EXPRESSION: Intellect, Thought,
Communication
SPIRIT KEEPER: Eagle(M)/Owl(F)
HUMAN CYCLE: Birth
CREATIVITY: New Beginnings,
Activation, Inspiration
COLOUR: Yellow/Green
MINERAL: Citrine

SOUTH

SEASON: Summer
ELEMENT: Water
ASPECT: Emotional
EXPRESSION: Emotions, Feelings, Nurturing,
Innocence, Humility
SPIRIT KEEPER: Frog(M)/Dolphin(F)
HUMAN CYCLE: Childhood
CREATIVITY: Development, Nurture, Protect
COLOUR: Blue
MINERAL: Amethyst

**NORTHERN
HEMISPHERE**

Summer
N

Autumn W

E Spring

**SOUTHERN
HEMISPHERE**

S
Winter

to see far in all directions, it is a metaphor that allows you to see in all directions in your life. The kinds of vegetation and terrain around your spot will all contribute to your experience. Sitting in a desert can feel purifying and expanding. A Quest under tall trees on soft moss can feel nurturing and supportive. A strong oak tree near your vision spot can help you to tap in to your innate strength and power. A creek flowing nearby can bring the qualities of inspiration and intuition. Take time and do a little research to find the right general area for you.

Finding the Specific Location for your Quest

After you have decided the general area for your Quest, the next step is to find the exact location. The best way to do this is first go to the area you have chosen and take some time to still your mind and relax. When you are relaxed your intuition becomes stronger. Turn slowly in all directions and see if there is one particular direction that seems to pull you. Walk slowly and deliberately in that direction, feeling relaxed and at ease. The more effort you put in to your walk and the more you 'try' to find the right location, the more difficult it becomes. Just relax. Breathe deeply, enjoy being in nature. Don't consciously decide where you want to go, just walk in a natural way as if you were going on a wonderful afternoon stroll. This kind of walking will usually direct you to the perfect spot for your Quest. The next step is to locate the exact centre for your circle. To do this, stand in the area you have chosen, close your eyes and notice what you are feeling. Do you feel comfortable? Do you feel energised and strong? Then move a few feet away and do the same thing. As you continue this process, by elimination you will discover the exact centre of the circle that is best for you.

Sometimes the search for the location for your Quest can be as enlightening as the Vision Quest itself. Jaap de Kreek, a Dutch advertising executive, wrote telling me about his search for his Quest location.

I had known the spot for more than twenty years. [In my med-itations and dreams I had seen] a sloping meadow sur-rounded with high trees, giving a wide view over a bay. In the middle of this stood one tree with its feet [roots] covered with soft moss. I had seen this spot often when I was on the edge of falling asleep. And when I was breaking through the bushes of Sacred Island, looking for a place where I could create my Vision Circle, I saw it again. But this time it was real. Right before my eyes . . . the slope, the tree, the bay, the moss, exactly as I had dreamed it. There was even already a beautiful circle of stones, just where it ought to be. Damn! Somebody had already marked the place as if it was their own. Well, I was prepared to fight for this spot [that had appeared to me so often in my dreams].

Behind me I heard a timid, 'Hello.' [I turned and saw] the only woman in the group that I didn't like. She had come to claim this place that she had found the day before.

[I thought,] 'The hell with you. I'm not going. I don't like you. I'm not giving up. Once again, a woman wants to send me away.' Angry emotions flashed through me. And then suddenly, I had a realisation. I recognised that I had the opportunity to release an old emotional pattern regarding

women. In that moment, I decided to let the woman have 'my' spot.

[I thought to myself,] 'Woman. I don't like you. I will never like you. But you gave me a present. You offered me the chance to look straight through myself to my ego.'

I walked back into the bushes. In a small basin was a boulder, broken into two pieces. There I wanted to sit for a while and recuperate from the shock. While my thoughts still heaved on the waves of my emotions, I saw that the boulder and I were surrounded by trees. Behind the branches glimmered the bay.

Two years later [I decided to go] to Sacred Island for my second Vision Quest. [I thought,] 'Now I can finally take the opportunity to take possession of my dream spot for my Quest.' At last I was sitting on the moss. My moss. I was happy. Then behind me I heard a timid 'Halloo.' A shy lady asked me if there was by chance another good spot in the area where she could create her vision circle.

'No, there is none,' I told her with certainty. I could see the disappointment in her eyes. Then I heard another voice [come out of my mouth and] say, 'But if you want, you can take this one.' I couldn't believe it. Was it really me who said this?

[But] while she was positioning herself on the spot that I knew by heart, I leaned on a broken boulder and slowly and contentedly felt myself melt into the womb of Mother Earth.

It's valuable to observe the thoughts, feelings and experiences you have while finding your spot. They can be significant and can give you powerful insights into yourself. Mervi Jakonen, a chiropodist from Finland, wrote to me about finding her location and what she gained from the search.

I panicked when I tried to find the right place for my Quest. You had advised me to look for the signs but I didn't see any. When I had asked you, 'How much time do I have to find my place?' you said, 'How much do you need?' [I couldn't find my place and] I was desperate when I realised that I had only one hour before dark to find my spot. I went to the forest, talked to the trees and asked them to help me. Nothing happened. I ran through the woods, talking to myself, knowing that I had to find some place. Then I gave up. Suddenly I realised what you really meant. It wasn't about finding the 'place', it was about finding 'when' I was ready. As soon as I had this realisation, I went straight to my place. I felt peace at that moment . . . and also a little stupid for tearing around through the woods. I had wanted a Vision Quest spot that was close to the sea, near a big tree and so that I could see the sunset and the clear sky at night. As soon as I was ready, my spot appeared. It was easy.

You do not need to struggle to find the perfect place. When you can still you mind, as Mervi did, and find sacred space inside yourself, it becomes easy to find sacred space outside yourself.

The earth has a living force within it. Your life force is constantly interacting with the living spirit within the earth. There are places on the earth where you are strengthened and places where you are weakened. They are not the same for everyone. Once a woman wanted to take me to her sacred spot in nature. She was very excited about showing it to me. We hiked for roughly a mile and then we had to push through dense vegetation for about twenty minutes. Finally we broke out of the brush into a small opening. A tree with thick foliage and low-lying branches created a shady covering of a small area that had a very small spring flowing through it. When we arrived, her entire energy field expanded and she looked more vibrant and radiant than I had ever seen her. I could see that the land was sustaining her. However, my energy began to dip and sag until I was exhausted and had difficulty making my way back down the trail. The location on the land that energised her, depleted me. It wasn't a bad spot or a good spot. It just interacted with her energy in a different way than it did with mine.

Creating your Sacred Circle

Usually a medicine wheel circle for a Vision Quest is made from stones, but it can also be created with the materials that are in the surrounding area, perhaps twigs or sticks or pine cones if there are no stones. Sometimes a Vision Quest circle is made of four twigs stuck upright in the earth with pieces of coloured cloth tied to them to represent the four directions. In some traditions tobacco is used to help create the sacred circle. It is used in many Native American ceremonies, for it is thought to be a medium of communication with the unseen ones, and is sacred to the Creator in all its forms. Vision seekers place a small pinch of tobacco in the centre of a one- to two-inch square of cloth, which is tied with string to make a small pouch. Bundles of these are tied together and strung around the periphery of the sacred Vision Quest circle. This helps to sanctify and energise the circle. There are many different ways and different materials to use to create your wheel; however, the materials that are used for your medicine wheel are less important than the respect you give to the entire process.

The Power of Stones in a Medicine Wheel

Ancient medicine men and women understood the power of stones and often used them in ceremonies and rituals because they believed that they contained living spirits with healing properties. Though rocks seem inanimate, they were thought to be no less alive than the wild rose opening to the morning sun or the deer grazing in a mountain meadow. Even the most guarded sceptic cannot deny the feeling created by the stones and rocks in their environment. Who is not moved by the power exuding from a magnificent boulder perched high on an ocean cliff as it defies harsh north winds? And who has not felt comforted just by holding a water-worn stone that fits perfectly in one's hand?

Creating your medicine wheel with stones will give your circle a sense of strength, stability and groundedness. The way you search for the stones, the specific stones you choose, and how you relate to those stones are all very important. In order to understand why stones are used for a sacred circle for your Vision Quest it helps to gain a perspective of the energy available within the mineral kingdom. Some Native people believe that there is a living spirit in each stone and they call stones and rocks 'stone people'.

In many aspects Taoist philosophy mirrors Native American kindredship with stones. Kio Jo-hsu, a Taoist Chinese painter in the T'ang Dynasty said:

He who is learning to paint must first still his heart, thus to clarify his understanding and increase his wisdom. In stilling the heart an individual can become one with the elements of nature, the great creative forces of the Tao and its processes. To clarify understanding and increase wisdom means a contemplative attention to all of nature's changes in order gradually to gain a sense of the permanent and significant. In estimating people, their quality of spirit (chi) is as basic as the way they are formed; and so it is with rocks, which are the framework of the heavens and of earth, and also have chi. This is the reason rocks are sometimes spoken of as 'roots of the clouds'.[1]

Native and ancient people saw a world beyond the material and the tangible and that is why they acknowledged the living spirit in rocks.

Where Do You Find Your Stones?

It's best to collect stones from the area where you will be embarking on your Vision Quest; however if there are no stones in that area you may bring stones from elsewhere. But please do not take stones from sacred sites. For example, many people have travelled to the interior of Australia to visit a sacred aboriginal site, Ayers Rock (called Uluru by the Aborigines), and have taken rocks back home with them. The Pitjantjatjara aboriginal people feel that those rocks belong to Uluru, which is a sacred 'dreaming' site, and have requested that any stones taken be returned home. A Chinese painter, Lu Ch'ai, talks about the living spirit of stones when he said that there is a kinship among rocks. 'Small rocks near water are like children gathered around with arms outstretched toward the mother rock. On a mountain that is a large rock, the elder, that seems to reach out and gather the children about him.'

If you live near the sea you might comb the beaches for your stones. Stones that have been smoothed and polished by the motion of the surf carry power from the depths of the ocean. Their spirit speaks of wide expansive skies, deep blue sea and the surging changes of surf and sand. The stones found inland have a completely different energy. Stones found near roots of trees or along the base of cliffs have the spirit of the ancient land. Their spirit carries a richness of the dark loam of Mother Earth and her primordial secrets. Stones found in inland riverbeds and streams carry the fluid-flowing energy of water as well as the strength of the earth. Every stone carries the energy of its past and the area where it is found.

How to Choose Your Stones

Each stone affects your energy field in a different way. When you randomly pick up a stone from the earth you are intuitively tapping in to the inherent beneficial energy within that particular stone. Each stone that you choose for your sacred circle affects the energy of the circle in a specific and unique way. As strange as it might sound, when you find stones for your medicine wheel, it's important first to ask permission to take them. There is a subtle yet powerful balance of energy on our planet and the mineral realm is an important contribution to that balance. Even changing the location of one stone can affect the pattern of energy flows throughout the land. Some stones need to stay where they are, so it's important to ask if it is all right to take a stone. Even if you feel a bit silly, as you hold your stone tap in to your intuition and imagine that you are carrying on a dialogue with the stone. Asking permission can be as simple as closing your eyes and asking, 'May I take you for my medicine wheel?' When the response comes, honour it. I find that most stones accept the invitation.

Whenever you move a stone from one place to another, inwardly acknowledge to the stone why it is being taken from its living place (this also helps you clarify your intention for your retreat). In addition, it's important when you take a stone for your sacred circle to leave an offering such as tobacco or cornmeal or some token of thanks. I know of a Blackfoot Indian who leaves shiny copper pennies when he takes something from nature. Though this is not low-impact camping ('take only pictures, leave only footprints'), it gives credence to the native tradition of honouring that which is taken from nature. If you have nothing tangible to leave, then in your mind offer words of thanks and gratitude. If possible, return your stones to the location where you found them after you have completed your Vision Quest.

Trance Walk to find Medicine Wheel Stones

When I was young, I was taught a particular kind of walking done by the Cherokees that I call Trance Walk. It is a valuable technique to use if you are having difficulty locating your stones. To Trance Walk to locate stones, stand with both feet stable and firm on the earth. You can wear shoes while doing this, if you want, although it's important to feel an emotional or energetic connection to the earth. Begin taking very deep full breaths that centre in your lower abdomen. This means when you inhale your abdomen expands, and when you exhale your abdomen contracts. As you continue these breaths, lower your eyelids, leaving them open just enough so that you can still see. Then place your awareness in your diaphragm area as you hold an intention of gathering stones for your circle. By doing this you are putting out the 'call' to be led to just the right stones for your circle.

Some people say they feel a sensation that seems like a tug or pull on their diaphragm area and some people just find themselves walking without any conscious decision to do so. As you walk, hold the thought of the particular qualities of the stone that you want to place on the wheel. For example, if you are looking for a stone to place in the south (which represents water) of your wheel, you might spend a moment connecting to the element of water and then say within yourself, 'Spirit of the South, Spirit of Water, direct me to a stone that will help me connect to the element of water during my Quest.' Sometimes it will seem like a stone is beckoning to you or sometimes it will seem shinier or brighter than the stones around it. I've seen stones that even seem to glow from within and I know that these stones will bring power and grace into my circle.

It is a good idea to obtain the four cardinal stones first. Thus the first stone will call forth the Spirit of the East, followed by the south, west and north. Once you have your four directional stones then you can Trance Walk for the intervening stones.

Feeling a Connection with your Stones

Once you have chosen your 'stone people' spend time with them before laying them in your circle, to understand and feel their power, beauty and grace. It is even possible to enter into the consciousness of these special rocks. Entering the awareness of animate and inanimate objects is one of the secrets of the shaman. Using methods similar to ancient mystic travellers, you can tap the spirit power of stones. It is important to do this before you create your sacred circle, for it brings you into closer commune with the stones that will form it.

To experience the living spirit within a stone, take it and hold it in front of you. Really look at it. Observe the mountains and valleys of its surface. Feel the texture and temperatures as you explore the surface with your fingers. Close your eyes and feel every corner and crevice of the surface. Breathe deeply, still your mind and imagine that you are entering into the centre of the stone's mass. As you embark on this imaginary journey, notice how you feel as you penetrate into the centre of the stone. Do you feel still and strong? Do you feel powerful and expansive? Every rock will have a different energy and will allow you a different experience.

Now imagine that you are actually becoming the stone and observe how it feels. Every stone is a unique spirit with a particular vibration of light and sound and its own story to tell. For example, a quartz crystal has a very different energy from a granite riverbed stone and turquoise is very different from obsidian. Quartz is light, bright and has a transmitting energy. A riverbed stone is grounding and strong.

Turquoise is porous and flowing, whereas obsidian is dense, solid and intense. Let yourself imagine or be aware of the story that dwells within each stone. Native American healers knew how to speak to stones and what particular influence each stone would have. They would specifically choose stones that created beneficial effects for the purpose they desired.

When you are surrounded by stones that you have specially chosen for your Quest, these 'stone people' stand around you like silent guardians with their ancient wisdom and timeless strength. It's important that you feel safe and protected on your Quest. The stones you have made friends with, and feel a connection to, will help create a circle of power around you. The 'stone people' become your friends and companions through the day and night. They will stand guard over you, bringing their rich grounding connection to Mother Earth while you are on your Quest.

Constructing your Sacred Circle

The centre of all medicine wheels is symbolic of the Creator, so the centre of your circle is important. Sometimes the centre is immediately apparent and sometimes you may need to spend time using your intuition to 'feel' where the exact spot is. Once you have decided on the centre it is important to declare your intention. For example, you might say, 'May Grandmother Earth below and Grandfather Sky overhead fill this place with energy and love as I create my Sacred Circle for my Vision Quest.' Sprinkle a little cornmeal (which symbolises protection and abundance) or tobacco (which is sacred to the Creator), and give a prayer of thanks in the centre of your circle.

If you want your circle to be fairly symmetrical here is a way to do it. Put a stick into the earth in the centre of your circle. Attach a string or cord half the length of the diameter of your circle to your stick. This means if you want a six-foot circle, tie a three-foot string to the stick. Then attach another stick to the other end of the string and etch a circumference in the dirt with it. This will make your medicine wheel a consistently even circle. It is not absolutely necessary, however, to make your medicine wheel an exact circle. Some terrains make an exact circle very difficult to create. The most important thing is to acknowledge within yourself that your sacred circle, no matter what form or shape it takes, is symbolic of the sacred circles within all life.

Make your circle bigger than your height so that you can comfortably lie down in it. (I like to use an eight–ten foot diameter.) One Vision Quester inadvertently made her circle shorter than her height which meant that she could only sit up in it rather than lie down. After a day of this, she realised that in life she was always creating self-limiting situations for herself and then complaining about her own self-imposed confines. She decided to make a new template for her life and thus she remade her circle so that she could move and lie down in it with ease. With this symbolic act, she realised that she could create a life for herself that was freer and less confined.

After you have decided on the shape, the next step is to clear the space. If there are small stones or sticks in the area, you can clear them out of the circle. In the creation of your circle, every act is sacred. Build your circle with awareness and reverence. Once the area is cleared, ascertain what direction is east. You can do this with a compass; however, the easiest way if you don't have a compass is to establish where the sun rises.

The ceremony of creating the circle brings power and clarity into your life. As you lay each stone or twig in your medicine wheel, you are enacting a ritual. When you call the elements into your circle, you will be honouring the different cycles in your life. Start by taking the stone that symbolises the east and ask that the Spirit of Air and the East fill your sacred circle. Place this stone in the easternmost area of the perimeter of your circle. Step back and feel energy filling your circle. Continue by placing the south stone, followed by the west stone and the north stone. With each step be aware that not only are you creating a physical circle, you are also creating a circle of energy. Each step of the creation process is calling power into your circle.

Your four cardinal stones represent the four elements and the four directions. These are laid out to form the perimeter of the circle. Allow equal space between each of the four major stones. In between these major stones, position the others, using as many stones as feels best to you. Remember, however, each stone that you place around your circle is bringing a very special energy into your circle. Each stone represents the transition from one quadrant of your life to another. The stone circle represents the pathway from one aspect of your life to another. Your placement of the stones is an affirmation that the transitions in your life are easy and flowing.

Take time setting up your wheel. This is a sacred tool so

treat the circle with respect. You are creating a womb or cocoon of energy with every aspect of the creation of your circle. When your circle is complete, stand back from it and see if it feels right. If it doesn't, spend time making whatever adjustments you need to until it does feel right.

When you have finished, give thanks. Thank the earth for providing such a special place for your Quest. Thank the surrounding vegetation and trees for giving loving support for your Quest. Ask for assistance from the Living Spirit in the surrounding area and give thanks for the beauty and love that is given from nature and from the realm of Spirit.

For some, the creation of the medicine wheel can be as meaningful as the Vision Quest itself. Rick Mauricio, a lighting engineer from Britain, had a vision while seeking and creating his power spot.

The Vision Quest for me was very much about finding my purpose in this life . . . I allowed myself to be drawn deep into the wood to find my spot. Once I reached a particular place, I found I could not advance past it in any direction. I didn't like the place. The air was thick with mosquitoes, flies and bugs but everything pointed to this being the place for me. Even though the area was filled with bushes and undergrowth, I had a feeling that this was where I was meant to be. The air was teeming with bugs, but the moment I created my sacred circle, all the insects stayed outside it! In fact, none entered until I dismantled my circle the next evening.

Once I stepped inside my circle I felt what seemed to be a powerful energy emitting up from the earth. It was just north of the centre of the circle. It wasn't there before I created the circle as I didn't feel it when I was clearing the ground. It must have emerged after the circle was complete. I was completely amazed by what I was feeling and moved my hand over the boundaries of the energy. Every time my hand got near it, I could feel a tingling in my fingers and palm.

To try to understand what was occurring, I dropped a leaf over the spot. The leaf swayed and danced in the air and then eventually fell. I rationalised that the leaf could have caught a breeze so I next decided to try a twig. The same thing happened. Again I rationalised that the twig was light so maybe it was a breeze that caused it to seem to hang in the air. I then tried a stone. Remarkably, the stone also danced and swayed and didn't land in the place it should have.

Dusk was approaching. I lay down next to the earth to see if I could understand what could cause this unusual phenomenon. In the failing light I saw a few small stones near the energy spot. I picked them up and moved them around in the palm of my hand. They began to emit light! As I stared closer at them in my hand I started to see them as stars. As the remaining daylight disappeared, I looked up and I could see a point of light through the trees. As I looked closer it looked like a great circle of light, almost like a medicine wheel.

There were points along the circumference that had bursts of light shooting in and out of the circle, like the points of a medicine wheel. I realised these shifting patterns of light represented the changes in my life. As the points lengthened and shortened, changing themselves, I realised that I could change myself. I then had the profound realisation that we can change anything and everything in a twinkling of an eye. It was at that point that my name came to me . . . Shifting Star. It is both *who I am and what I'm capable of. This was a momentous moment in my life. The energy vortex in my sacred circle, the glowing stones and shifting light were all gifts to me that showed me the limitless possibilities of being here on Mother Earth in this life. The most reassuring aspect to arise since my Vision Quest is that the way I respond to my world is always changing and I with it. Each day and moment is a Vision Quest for me.*

Tessa Dace, a developer for affordable housing in South Africa, talked about the beauty of the creation of her circle.

I slowly set about the ritual of forming my circle. Selecting a large rock I spoke first to the east, and [dedicated the rock to] the air, the spring, mental thought and the gateway to my circle. I asked for help in my Quest for inner knowledge, as I ceremoniously placed the rock on the ground. [I placed] another rock in the south, for the summer, the water and emotions. I knew I would need assistance here! I placed another rock for the west, for fire, for autumn and for energy beneath the handsome sturdy pine with its strong masculine trunk. A last stone I placed beneath a wizened old tree at the north, symbolising earth, winter and abundance. The spaces between I filled with smaller rocks, pieces of driftwood and bark, each placed with reverence in my private ceremony. Addressing all my relations, in the Native American custom, I entered my circle from the east and lay down on the moss bed. My precious drum, so newly finished, hung to dry next to my head. I could almost hear the deep voice it would have. My dream catcher, sage bundle and tobacco pouch becoming an impromptu altar.

Feeling the words I had just spoken in my sacred ceremony so very close to my heart, I stared out to sea.

Prior to Entering your Circle for your Quest

Prior to entering your medicine wheel, purify and consecrate yourself by 'smudging'. Smudging or sage cleansing is a sacred ritual used for purification and preparation for ceremonies. To smudge, carefully light a sage bundle (if you do not have a sage bundle you may use incense) and take the smoke in your hands and 'wash' over your hair and head (to think only pure thoughts), eyes (to see the truth), ears (to hear the truth), throat (to speak with clarity and truth) and heart (to give and receive love freely). Be very careful with matches and fire to avoid fire hazard. If you are doing your Quest without matches or sage, take your hands and repeat the same symbolic 'washing' motions but without the smoke. (Important: in an area of high fire risk *do not* use matches, or make a fire or smoke.) A symbolic smudging can be as potent as actually using smoking herbs, if done with intent and love. There is power in symbolic gestures.

Before entering your circle, hold in your mind's eye your overall intention for your Quest. Taking the time to concentrate on your intention for your Quest is important. Perhaps you desire to gain clarity about your future path or want to resolve a relationship or wish to evaluate a career decision. Where intention goes, energy flows, so placing your intention on the area in your life you wish to change will help energy flow in that direction.

After you have focused on your intent for your Quest, a prayer is then offered to the Creator to ask for a blessing during the Quest. The best prayers come straight from your heart, honestly and sincerely. This is a very holy time. You are literally calling Spirit into your circle; calling your spirit helpers, guides, spirit guardians and angels to surround and fill your circle. When you have finished with your prayers, give thanks to the Creator.

Entering your Medicine Wheel

The beginning of the wheel is the east (because the sun rises in the east) so always enter and leave the wheel through the eastern portion of the circle. When you set foot in your circle you may immediately notice a difference in the energy inside and outside, because you are entering a vortex of energy that has been created by careful attention and love. Many times Vision Questers have recounted stories of watching animals walking towards their circle and then carefully walking around the circumference, even when the stones were so small as not to be differentiated by the area. Your medicine wheel is a sacred space where you can inter-face with the universe and often animals can feel this.

Candace created a beautiful medicine wheel for her Quest. It was in the centre of a large meadow in the Cascade Mountains. There weren't any large rocks in the area so she had gathered gravel-sized stones to create her circle. On the second day of her Quest, she had to go to a spring to get more water. It was some distance from her circle so she was gone about an hour. When she returned she saw that there were numerous hoof marks of range cattle completely sur-rounding her circle, yet not one hoof mark was inside her circle. The cattle had intuitively felt the energy of her sacred space and respected it by not stepping inside the circle. Other people on Quests have had the experience of certain animals being attracted to the energy of their medicine circles. Sometimes an animal entering your circle might be the bearer of a message, which could be a part of your vision. The energy you create by your intention in building your circle, both conscious and unconscious, helps to determine what will happen as a result. The important thing is to be open to all the signs and information which come to you.

Once you have entered the medicine wheel, either sit or stand in the centre and take a moment to be still. Listen. Close your eyes and take seven deep breaths (one breath for each direction, one breath for the energy above, one for the energy below and one for the centre or the Creator). Take as much time as you like to centre yourself and become deeply relaxed. Face the east and allow yourself to feel a connection to the Spirit of the East. Shift positions to face each quadrant: east, south, west and north. (In the southern hemisphere face east, north, west and south.) Hold the intention for your Quest within your thoughts. As you face each cardinal point imagine drawing energy from that quadrant; focus and examine your intent, viewed from the perspective and power of each direction.

Listen and perceive the power of the direction you face. It may manifest itself as light, colour, sound, an insight or a feeling. When finished with each direction, move your awareness to the centre of the circle. Feel the energies from each direction spiralling towards the middle of the wheel; in this vortex of energy, send your prayers up to Spirit. You can now bring everything that you are going to use on your

Quest into the circle, e.g. sleeping bag and water. (Remember to enter and leave through the east.) Every time you cross over the threshold, say 'I do this for the good of all beings,' as a way to remind yourself of the value of what you are doing. Some individuals say, 'To all my relations' which is a similar sentiment. You are now ready to begin your Quest.

Gael Edmeades, a Reiki Master from South Africa, wrote about creating her circle.

The day we all had been waiting for was almost upon us. Morning dawned and it was raining! Groaning silently to myself at the thought of sitting out there in the rain for two days but, ever resourceful, making a quick raid on the kitchen for black plastic bags which were to be used as roof and ground-sheet, I prepared my medicine wheel. My spot was a circle within a circle of stones within a circle of trees. What could be more magic than that? I set out my stones and feathers to mark the south, west, north and then closed the east after inviting the ancestors and guardians in. I lay down on my stomach in the middle of my medicine wheel and felt every bone and muscle and sinew dissolve as I blended with the healing power of the earth. I had no boundaries, neither physical, mental, nor emotional and I felt the heartbeat of the earth . . . and I was one with it.

Creating a Medicine Wheel Indoors

Though the opportunity to embark on a Quest in nature can bring a wonderful dimension to your retreat, not everyone has the opportunity or inclination to Quest in nature.

Therefore, you can create a Quest indoors. Your medicine wheel can be created using the above information for finding and placing your stones or you can make your indoor circle with special objects. For example, because of health concerns, one woman decided to create her medicine wheel indoors. She had collected a number of feathers over the years so she decided to use her precious feathers to make her circle. She took the feathers and through a process of meditation decided which of them should be placed in the positions of east, south, west and north. After this, she used the remainder of the feathers to create the circle, in much the same way that smaller 'stepping stones' are used in a stone circle. She had a very successful Quest and afterwards said that she had felt that her circle was surrounded by the wings of angels.

Rocks or twigs can be brought in from outdoors to create an indoor sacred circle. Evergreen boughs and needles may also be placed to form the wheel. Whatever objects have significance for you, and are readily available, can be used for this purpose, using the steps outlined above.

In the world today sacred space is being forgotten. However, deep within the recesses of the mind, there is a primal memory of the power of the sacred circle. That ancient, though elusive, memory has the ability to activate a conditioned response that connects you to the majesty of past Quests. It is an act of power to create sacred circles which help to remind us how to live in a sacred way. The medicine wheel can take you back in safety to the simplest forms of living. It also can bring you back lovingly to the present, without the complexity of social norms telling you what you need in order to be full and complete; it is already gained in wholeness within the context of the circle. Casting the sacred circle can help remind you who you are and why you are here. This is the power of the Quest within the circle.

4 *What Do You Do on a Vision Quest?*

Your needs, as well as what you hope to achieve on your Quest, will help determine what you do on your Quest. Some Quests may be aimed at addressing various aspects of life and have a specific agenda. For someone who is very goal-oriented, this kind of Quest may be just one more thing to cross off on the 'To Do List' of life. For this kind of individual sometimes the best thing to do on a Vision Quest is *nothing*. Just sit. Just BE. There is nothing you have to do or accomplish. Be still. Surrender. Watch. Listen. Feel. Be. Move towards acceptance of absolutely everything that occurs. Be the observer. Be in the present moment without judgment or expectations and without trying to accomplish anything.

For another type of individual the way to self-discovery is to have a direction or focus for their Vision Quest. If you are one of those individuals, I have created a five-step journey that you may want to use as a guideline for your time alone in nature.

Step 1. Examine your Life
Step 2. Face Your Fears and Release Attachments
Step 3. Tapping into the Spirit Power within
Step 4. Giving Thanks
Step 5. Calling for a Vision

Step 1. Examine your Life

Relive your Life

Go through your entire life remembering, experiencing and accepting as much as your can. (If you are using a journal, you may want to write it all down.) Try to remember every possible detail of your life, starting from early childhood to the present time. If you find you are having trouble remembering details from some period, simply jot down what you can remember. Doing this often primes the pump so that more memories come flowing out to fill in the gaps. Don't get stuck in any one place. Just write as much as you can remember and keep going. Review your past actions and pay particular attention to your feelings. If you do find yourself reliving deeply felt emotions, it's important to honour and respect those feelings. However, if you find yourself getting bogged down in an old emotional repeating pattern, become the observer. Try to observe the situation from an impartial viewpoint. Janice spent half a day, on her Quest, reliving her anger at her older sister. She thought over and over again 'I'll never forgive her. Never. Never!' Although there is value in bringing repressed emotions to the surface, sometimes negative emotions can be like a scratched record which keeps repeating over and over again. Janice kept repeating the same scenario in her mind, which was not productive. I suggested that she observe the situation from a detached perspective. When she did this she was able to understand not only the situation with her sister, but also a series of repeating relationship patterns in her life.

Exercise: Witness your Life

Re-experience your life in its totality, and at the same time watch it unfold. Become the objective witness. Do not judge; just observe. Notice patterns that continue to reoccur during your life. Notice recurring issues. What has been really significant in your life?

When you look back at your life, often there are only a few things that really stand out. Sometimes it seems as if the rest of the time has been waiting for those things to happen. It is not our monumental projects and great plans that are the real stuff that life is made of but often the space between these events, the ordinary everyday moments of life, which contain the crucial and potent moments of soul. These are often the moments from which our definitions of self arise.

Exercise: Turning Points in Life

What are the main events in *your* life? Do you spend your life waiting for the future, rather than living each moment fully? What are the turning points in your life?

What is your Essence? What is your Theme?

There is a prevailing theme that runs through your life, just as there is a prevalent essence of you that has woven its way through your personal history. What has your life's theme been? What is the unique essence of you?

Sandy, a florist from Utah, detailed her life history in a

journal she took on her Quest. As she wrote, she began to notice a recurring lifelong pattern of being involved in relationships where she felt smothered by the affection of others. As she explored her life's theme, she realised that freedom was extraordinarily important to her; the theme of her entire life was based on gaining physical, emotional and spiritual freedom. When she examined the moments in her life that were truly important to her, they all seemed to carry a theme of freedom. Each major incident in her life revolved around freedom: the time when she got into a fight with her parents about getting her driving licence, the time when she picketed a government building for suppressing freedom of the press, and the time her boyfriend wanted her to exclude other friends from her life. As she further explored her life, she wanted to find her essence. She asked her inner voice, 'What is my essence?' This is what she heard: 'I heard an inner voice speak clearly, "You are Truth." When I said the words to myself, "I am Truth," I felt fantastic. I knew I had touched my essence.' Sandy realised that when she spoke her 'truth', she was 'free'. Your essence manifests through the theme of your life, therefore her essence ('truth') was manifested through her life theme of 'freedom'.

Exercise: What is your Theme?

What is your essence? What is the theme of your life? What is essentially unique about you? What have been consistent motifs throughout your life? What do you constantly struggle with? In what area of your life do you continually gain your triumphs?

Consequences of your Life Choices and your Probable Future

Every act creates consequences. Even the simple act of picking up a small stone and tossing it into a lake can potentially affect the outcome of history. (The stone could startle a large fish, which swims into a net, that is caught by the fisherman, who takes it home to his village clan leader, who invites the neighbouring clan leader for a fish meal, who chokes on a fish bone, which starts a war, which affects the course of history.) Do not let the fact that your actions have consequences inhibit you from taking action in your life. Just do the best that you can. Even the smallest act taken with a loving heart can make a big impact in your life. Set your sights on the direction you want to walk, and to the best of your ability walk that path. Then relax and know that your life is working out the way that it should. (Don't worry if all your acts aren't pure hearted – nobody is completely loving. Most of your mistakes are not going to cause catastrophes!) Take responsibility for your actions but don't get bogged down in guilt or fear.

Because you are in a circle of power, the small positive steps that you take during your Vision Quest can have a dramatic effect on your future. All life is interdependent and every act creates a ripple in the fabric of time. Everything you think or do sets your future in motion. Every single thought and action has an effect on your future or has a result in your life. You *can* re-create your future during the Vision Quest. During your Quest you can set an energy in motion that can literally alter the course of your probabilities, and can even change your destiny.

Exercise: Probability Pattern of your Future

Given your past thoughts and actions, what is your current destiny? In your imagination, project yourself into your future. Given the probabilities of your past history, and given your subconscious programming, what is in store for your future? Contemplate travelling to your probable future. One year? Five years? Seven years? Ten years? Twenty years? Thirty? Forty and beyond? Are you happy with what you see? Do you feel satisfied with the probability patterns of your future?

Go forward in time to just before your death. Imagine yourself sitting in a rocking chair looking back on your life. Are there any regrets? What changes would you make? People very rarely regret what they did do, but often regret what they didn't do. What would you change if you could do it all over again? Is there anything in your present life you need to change to assist your potential future? Examine how that change will alter every aspect of your life and make sure you are at peace with that. If you see anything in your probable future with which you are uncomfortable, picture it dissolving and then imagine how you can create a future you desire.

Examining your Relationships

Relationship to Self: Your Beliefs

It is enormously valuable to examine the relationships in your life, starting with your relationship with yourself. To discover the dynamics of your relationship with yourself begin by examining your beliefs. One of the most dynamic configurations of thought is a belief. A belief is a concept that you consider to be the truth. It can dictate the way you think and feel and can even impel the way you act. Your personal beliefs can cause you to attract particular situations and circumstances into your life. Whatever you believe has consequences. In fact, your beliefs can determine the outcome of your life.

'Core' beliefs are more influential than ordinary beliefs. They are beliefs that are generally so deep-seated that you're not even conscious of them, yet they have tremendous effect on your life. They are so instilled in you that they become a part of your 'ground of being', rather like gravity which you usually don't question or think about. It's just the way it is.

Subconsciously, we are constantly trying to validate our core beliefs. We feel the need to be 'right' about these beliefs so we subconsciously create a reality to justify our beliefs . . . *even if the beliefs are negative*. For example, Emilio had a core belief that dogs were dangerous. Even though consciously he realised that most dogs were not a problem, whenever he went for a walk dogs inevitably barked at him. He subconsciously projected fear whenever he approached a dog. Consequently dogs, sensing fear, would often react negatively to Emilio. This repeated unpleasant experience validated his deep inner belief that dogs are dangerous. Ron presents another example. He consciously really enjoyed the company of women; however every time Ron became intimate with a woman she would betray his trust. Upon examining his life, he realised that this pattern recurred through the years. Though he *consciously* believed that he could be intimate with women, he realised that he had a strong inner core belief that women couldn't be trusted.

Exercise: What are your Beliefs?

List as many conscious beliefs as you can, taking time to discern where they may have originated (from a parent, friend, family member, society, etc.). Are you happy with your beliefs? Then list your core beliefs. The quickest way to discover your core beliefs is to observe the reality with which you have surrounded yourself. Given that your core beliefs create your reality, which core beliefs would explain the reality of your life? After you have made your list, look it over and see if you are happy with all your core beliefs. What do your beliefs and core beliefs tell you about your relationship to yourself?

In one of Trees' Vision Quests she had the opportunity to begin to recognise and release a fundamental negative belief that she had held for a long time.

The first day I drank a lot of water. The second day I put the container at the tree with my ribbon to indicate that I wanted more water. When the sun was at its highest I thought it was time for someone to come with water ... but no water came. I prayed and sang ... and after a long time I left my circle to see if someone had left water in my container by the tree ... but still no water. I went back to my circle, crying all the way. In the past, every time I trusted someone, they betrayed me. They usually didn't do what they said they would do. I cried for a long time. It hurt so much.

Then I decided to leave my circle and go back to base camp to get water. I had to take action. I left my circle, checked the tree again, and went all the way to base camp. It was a long walk. On my way I saw many full water bottles belonging to other Questers. I thought perhaps the water had been brought, but another Quester took it. 'Are you coming back?' a Quester asked me. 'No, I need water now!' I replied. I had never been so direct and so angry.

When I got back to base camp I learned that water had already been brought, but one of the assistants still came back with me with more fresh water. On the way back to my circle so much anger came out of me. The funny thing is that when we came back to the tree the water was there, partially hidden by grass. In my circle I asked Great Spirit to forgive me for not trusting people. This lesson I will never forget. I also realised that I am responsible for myself.

When we are ready to release an old belief, we will often go out of our way (subconsciously) to create a similar situation that will allow the belief to surface so that it can be released. Hence, even though there *was* water available, Trees subconsciously chose not to see it so that her old belief of not trusting people could come to the surface.

When you sit in a sacred circle during your Quest, with no outside stimulus, it becomes much easier to see your belief patterns because there are fewer exterior circumstances to justify them. Normally when beliefs arise in our life they seem real because there is an external stimulus that seems to justify the belief. A person who believes that the world is an angry place will see angry people wherever they go, thus justifying their belief in an angry world. But when someone is sitting in a circle of stones in nature feeling angry it becomes more obvious where the emotion is coming from. Basically when you are in the circle . . . you are just sitting in a circle. Nothing more and nothing less. However, the sanctity of the circle offers the opportunity to *observe* your beliefs rather than acting them out. Here are some thoughts and the underlying beliefs that have arisen on Vision Quests.

- 'My circle isn't good enough. Everyone has a better circle than me.' (Belief: Everyone is better than me.)
- 'My location is wrong. Why did I choose this location? Now I'm stuck with my choice.' (Belief: I never make the right choice.)
- 'I'm sitting here all by myself feeling I'm abandoned. Why have they abandoned me?' (Belief: I'll always be abandoned in life.)
- 'I'm not doing my Vision Quest right.' (Belief: I never do anything right.)
- 'This isn't working.' (Belief: Nothing ever works out for me.)

When you can observe a belief, instead of acting on it, you can begin to loosen the hold that the belief has on you.

Gaining New Beliefs
We define ourselves by our beliefs; your life takes a 'shape' that's dictated by the beliefs that you hold. When you adopt a belief system that is dictated from the outside, you are

defined by another's form and, like a wrong-sized shoe, it can pinch. During your Quest you have the opportunity to relinquish old limiting beliefs and embrace new beliefs that empower you. You can actually re-engineer your consciousness. You have the opportunity to make radical changes in the thought patterns that have been running your life. You can do this by identifying your core beliefs, and then replacing them with more powerful ones. This is not a juxtaposing of one idea for another or an introduction of a new set of ideas in an old mind-set. It is actually a restructuring of the mind according to your conscious choice.

When you fully understand the beliefs which have been limiting your ability to live out your dreams and be all that you have always hoped you could be, then you can release them. There is tremendous power in realizing what your core beliefs are. For much of our lives we go around assuming that our underlying beliefs are an accurate reflection of reality instead of just our own individual perceptions. These perceptions are formed by many forces in our lives, but once we realize what they are and explore them fully, then we are finally ready to release the ones that don't work and replace them with assumptions which support and empower us.

Exercise: Restructuring Beliefs

As you discover your core beliefs, list them on the left-hand margin of a piece of paper. If you discover a belief that doesn't empower you, cross a line through it and next to it write a new core belief that is supportive and positive.

Exercise: Anchoring New Beliefs

After you have written down your desired new beliefs, it's important to anchor these new beliefs into your body and your subconscious. To do this, think of the new belief and imagine going into your body and finding a place that you might associate with this new belief. Place your left hand on that part of your body and imagine breathing into that part of your body at the same time as you are thinking of your new belief. This begins to imbed the new belief into your body. Every time you find the old limiting belief filtering back into your life, place your hand on your body and repeat the exercise.

For example, if you want to anchor the belief that 'I am a valuable person' into your energy field, you might decide that your chest will be the place in your body that you will use to anchor this belief. Place your left hand on your chest and think, 'I am a valuable person.' And then any time that a thought of lack of esteem occurs you would put your hand on your chest and say to yourself, 'I am a valuable person.' After a while the new belief replaces the old one.

Relationship to Self: Identification

You perhaps have heard the story about the elephant and the five blind men. When asked to describe an elephant the first blind man reached out and felt a leg and said, 'Oh, I known what an elephant is like. It is exactly like a tree trunk.' The second blind man felt the tail and said, 'Oh no, you are wrong. An elephant is exactly like a rope.' The third blind man touched an ear and said, 'An elephant isn't a tree trunk or a rope, it is like a lotus leaf.' The fourth blind man touched the tusk and said, 'Oh, my friends, you are mistaken. An elephant is made of bone.' And the fifth blind man touched the trunk and said, 'Everyone is wrong! I have touched the elephant and it is just like a snake.' Every man was right and yet what they experienced was only a part of the whole. We each have different identities that we take on at different times in life which are only a part of the whole.

Sometimes we identify with our body and sometimes with our possessions and sometimes with our family. A man who runs into a burning building to save his jewels is identifying more strongly with his material goods than with his body. A person who has lots of plastic surgery is often identifying the self with their body.

To begin to loosen the hold your identification has on you, examine your identity. Who are you? Write down everything that you think and feel you are. For example, Sarah wrote on her list: wife, mother, daughter, artist, cook, lover, and woman. These labels were the major identities that she took on during a day. Identities are not bad, they allow you to function in the world. However, they become difficult when you get lost in the drama and really believe that you are the role, instead of an actor who is only playing a role. When you awaken from this illusion, you realise that you are not the role. You are Spirit.

Exercise: Expanding Definition of Self

Expand your awareness to include everything that you can see from your Vision Quest site. Continue to expand your awareness to include the world and the universe and beyond. Really imagine that your personal borders expand far beyond your body. Continue to expand your awareness to include the world and the universe and beyond. This is an excellent exercise to expand your definition of self and to begin to lose a sense of self-importance. Self-importance is actually a limiting definition of self because it defines you as the circumstances of your life. You are actually so much more. When you expand your parameters of perception you begin to recognise, in the deepest place within you, the expansive divinity and majesty that dwells within you.

What is your joy?

In your self-assessment explore what gives you joy in life. What truly makes you happy? What do you lose yourself in so deeply that you aren't aware of time passing? When do you feel the most content? It's difficult to pursue happiness if you aren't clear what makes you happy. If you are unsure where to begin, start by going back into your childhood and find what gave you joy as a child. Even in the most dysfunctional childhood there are still moments of joy. Once you have found the essence of what has given you joy, see if there is a way to distil that into your life. Spend a moment imagining yourself feeling fulfilled and joyful.

Exercise: What Gives You Joy?

List all the times in your life when you truly felt happy. As you look over the list is there any common theme that runs through all the items? Describe the times, as a child, when you were happiest. Is there a commonality in these experiences of childhood joy?

Where is your power?

Power comes from reaching into your innermost being and finding and living your truth, without question and without hesitation. You glow with inner power when your words come straight from your heart. In life we are encouraged to live other people's expectations. We are conditioned to respond to situations based on the way that society dictates we should respond. However, when you reach into your soul with courage and focus, and interact with the world from that place of inner truth, you are powerful.

Exercise: Where is your Power?

List all the times in your life when you felt powerful? Is there any common theme that runs through all the items on the list? Describe the times in your childhood when you felt that you were in your power, as well as times when you felt empowered. Is there a commonality in these childhood experiences?

Relationship to Others

Past relationships

Every person who has been in your life is your teacher and healer. And this is true especially of the people with whom you have had the greatest difficulty. The Dalai Lama said that you don't learn tolerance from friends. Every person in your life has allowed you to learn and to grow in compassion and understanding as a human being. Truly every person you meet is 'an assignment from God'. In order to step into your future with strength and power, it is very important to begin to heal old emotional wounds and miscommunications with the people who have been in your life. Your Vision Quest is an excellent time to do this because of the energy and clarity that you can garner within yourself. There is a direct correlation between your ability to forgive others and your ability to forgive yourself. Forgiveness can heal.

Several years ago I was giving a seminar in Finland. A downtrodden man, who looked as if he had lived a hard life, came into the seminar room and sat near the back of the room. At the end of the seminar he came up to talk to me. His mien was completely changed. His deeply lined face was radiant and tears streamed down his cheeks. He explained that ten years earlier he had murdered his mother. He was sent to prison and was released after seven years. He said that although society had forgiven his crime, there wasn't a day, or an hour, or even a minute when he had forgiven himself. His life was filled with excruciating guilt. His every day was a living hell. He explained that, during one of the exercises during the seminar, he had 'seen' his mother. She came to him softly, radiating love and said, 'Son. You are forgiven. I love you.' He instantly felt a deep peace fill him and he felt a heavy burden drop from his shoulders. He said, 'I am now ready to live again.'

This is the power of forgiveness. Even if you have committed the most heinous act, it does not help you or anyone else to hold on to guilt. Everybody is worthy of redemption. It's important to forgive yourself. If someone has done something harmful to you, forgiveness doesn't necessarily mean that you need to forgive the act. Some acts can seem unforgivable. Forgiving the person, even if you can't forgive the act, can be very beneficial to you.

Exercise: Forgiveness

As you explore your life, locate those people who have wronged you and the people whom you have wronged. Who have you been unkind to and who has been unkind to you? Imagine yourself speaking or communicating with each of these individuals and really 'speaking your truth' to them. Then listen to them speak *their* truth to you. Imagine this inner dialogue until you reach some kind of resolve or understanding. Go through your life and honour all relationships. What haven't you communicated that you need to communicate? If there is someone to whom you haven't expressed your anger, rage, grief, bitterness, or resentment, then imagine expressing yourself to that person . . . and listen to what they have to share with you. Who do you need to forgive? Forgive them. If you just can't forgive them, then forgive yourself for *not* forgiving others.

Current relationships

Spend some time exploring your current relationships. Are you satisfied with them? Every person in your life is a reflection of some aspect of you. It is valuable to ascertain what quality each person represents within you. If you have some difficult relationships, the Vision Quest is an excellent place to begin to heal them. Sometimes a remarkable healing of relationships occurs immediately following a Quest.

Exercise: Significant People in your Life

List the important or significant people in your life on the left-hand column of a piece of paper. Next to each person's name write what you feel is their most prevalent quality. When you have finished, go down the list of qualities and see how they relate to you. Every person who is significant in your life represents an important aspect of yourself.

Exercise: Action Needed in your Life

Focus on each person who is important in your life. Is there any action that you need to take regarding that person? If there is, plan when and how you are going to implement the change. For example, Joe put his son down as one of his significant relationships. When he looked to see if there was any action he needed to take he realised he needed to spend more time with his son. He then decided to take him to a ball game when he returned from his Quest. If there is something that you need to change in a relationship, be sure to examine how that change will alter every aspect of your life and make sure you are at peace with that.

Relationship to your Parents

Your parents (or the people who raised you) have an irrevocable effect on you. Not only did they give you physical birth (if they were your biological parents), but they also gave birth to the early childhood conditioning that most likely continues to colour your perception of life. To discover your real self, it's helpful to know what beliefs you have acquired from your parents and to ascertain if those beliefs are appropriate for your life now. In addition, it's valuable to discover what your parents stand for and how that relates symbolically to your life. Your parents are not random. We each have chosen our parents. No matter whether they were 'good' parents or 'bad' parents, they nevertheless played a valuable role in your spiritual development.

Exercise: Relationship to Parents

How do you feel about your parents? How do you perceive they feel about you? Why do you think you chose these particular people? Do you feel complete with your parents? If not, what do you need in order to feel complete? What do you feel you didn't get from your parents when you were growing up? Often what you didn't receive emotionally from your parents is what you perceive you don't receive from your partner. What you didn't receive from your parents (e.g. love or trust or tenderness) can also be the gift you have to give to others.

Life Evaluation Questions

If you can't see the patterns in your life, it makes it difficult to change them. One way to see these patterns is to answer questions intended to reveal the underlying forces at play in your life. Here are questions that you might explore during your Quest. Of course, you don't need to answer them all. They are only given to highlight some areas of your life you might want to examine.

Your Relationship with Yourself

- Where are you now in your life physically, emotionally and spiritually?
- What does the purpose of your life seem to be?
- What have you been putting off in your life?
- What do you need to forgive yourself for?
- What gives you your greatest joy?
- What do you really want to do with your life?
- What is really important to you?
- What have you always dreamed of doing? Why haven't you done it?
- Do you have any habits or addictions or compulsions? Why do you think you have them?
- Do you have to struggle to get ahead or does life unfold easily for you?
- What are the things that you like best about yourself? What are the things that you dislike about yourself?
- What would you like to change about yourself? Can you accept yourself if you never change?
- Would you like to know exactly when you are going to die? How would your life change if you knew?
- What are you afraid of? What do you need to do to face or release your fears?

Your Relationship to Other People

- What don't you want others to know about you?
- What have you never told anyone?
- Are you afraid of anyone?
- Who do you feel closest to?
- What do you think other people think about you?
- When you need help, are you willing to ask for it?
- Who are your people?
- Can you take compliments without having to explain or demur and say that you don't really deserve it?
- What public person do you admire (and who do you dislike) the most and why? (Usually the qualities that you admire or dislike in another are the qualities within yourself that you subconsciously like or dislike.)
- Who are your teachers?
- Who is the most important person in your life? Are you happy with the relationship as it is? Is there anything you need to change or heal in this relationship?

Your Relationship to the Divine

- Who, what and where do you get your spiritual inspiration?
- What is your name for the Creator?
- Who or what do you think the Creator is?
- What is the purpose of the Creator in your life?
- What do you want the Creator to know about you?
- If you have conditions for the Creator in your life, what are they? Are you willing to let them go?
- What do you think the Creator feels about you?
- Do you think or feel that the Creator has a plan for you? What do you think it is?

- Are you willing to let go completely and allow the Creator to guide your life?

Your Communications

- Do you speak from your heart and say what's on your mind?
- Do you say yes when you mean no, and no when you mean yes?
- Do you say things that you don't really mean just to be polite?
- Do you talk negatively about people privately whom you are pleasant to in person?
- Do you listen when others are talking?
- Do you interrupt others in conversations?
- Do your words match your actions?

Your Relationship to Money

- Are you happy with how much abundance you have in your life?
- What are your core beliefs about money?
- Are you afraid of having (or not having) money?
- What would change in your life if you did have money?
- What wouldn't change in your life if you had more money?
- What was your parents' relationship to money?
- Do you believe that you have to work hard to have money?
- What are your judgments about rich and poor people?

Your Relationship to Sexuality

- Do you enjoy sex? Why or why not?
- Do you prefer the company of your own sex or the opposite sex?
- Are your best friends usually male or female?
- Do you have a recurring sexual fantasy? What would you think of someone else who had that same fantasy?
- What makes you most uncomfortable about sex?
- Is there anything with regard to sex that makes you feel guilty or ashamed?

Your Relationship to your Career

- What are your skills/gifts? Are you using these skills in your career?
- Are you doing what you *really* want to do with your life?
- Do you enjoy your work?
- What did you really enjoy doing as a child?
- If money were not an issue, what work would you do?
- What are your goals?
- Do you keep your commitments?
- Do you do what you say you are going to do? If not, why not?
- Do you take risks in your career?

Life Situation Questions

Here are some situation questions that can allow you a deeper insight into yourself. These questions don't have 'right' or 'wrong' answers. They are each aimed at allowing a deeper understanding of yourself. When answering these questions, imagine yourself in the situations and be aware of

how you would respond. Probe within yourself to understand why you would respond in a certain way. As you contemplate these questions, explore your values and see if they
came from your own life experience, from your family and
friends or even from past life experiences. Sometimes the
difficulty that arises from trying to answer these questions
can bring unresolved conflicts to the surface. Notice the
questions that you don't feel inclined to grapple with. For
example, notice if you avoid any question that concerns
death. The way you feel about a question can give you as
much insight into yourself as the answer itself. Your feelings
about the question can also be a sign of unresolved concerns
within your subconscious mind. Each question has underlying issues that can warrant deep soul-searching. Observing
the way you deal with these questions on your Vision Quest
is an excellent way for you to gain self-understanding.

- If you could live for ever in good health would you?
  Why or why not?
- If you could have five people with you as you were
  dying, who would you choose and why?
- If you only had one year to live, what would you do with
  your time? Would you change anything in your current
  life? Are you willing to make those changes without
  imminent death hanging over you? Why or why not?
- If you could have only one of your material possessions,
  what would it be and why?
- If you could spend the day with anyone in the world
  who would it be and why?
- It's late at night and while parking you slightly scratch
  the side of a new car. No one sees you. Do you leave a
  note?

- Are you always early, always on time or always late? How do you feel about people who are always early, on time or late?
- If you were given one million pounds what would you do with it? Ten million?
- If you could be any animal, what animal would you be? Why?
- If you are in an argument and you realise that you are wrong, do you admit it right away or do you keep defending your point of view?
- If you are walking down the street and find a brown paper bag filled with £10,000 in cash but no identification would you keep it or hand it in to the police? What if there was someone's name and address in it?
- You are given one million pounds to use for non-personal gain. What do you do with it?
- If you could have one perfect day, what would you do from the time you woke up until you went to sleep?
- If you came home from grocery shopping and realised that you were not charged for an item, would you compensate the store the next time you went? What if you noticed the mistake in the car park before you left?

Step 2: Face your Fears and Release Attachments

Facing your Fears

Facing fear takes courage. Most people would rather live a life within familiar confines than take a step to face the unknown realm where fear dwells. However, illness, weakness, fragmentation and isolation can result when you live with fear rather than face it because fear lowers your energy.

Facing fear can be terrifying. It can require enormous willpower to step through the veil of illusion that fear emits. And yet facing your fears can be the most empowering thing that you do in your life. Remarkably, you can overcome fears on your Vision Quest through a very simple technique. Simply imagine each fear in its worst possible scenario (even over-exaggerate it) and then, in your imagination, find a way either to overcome the situation or to accept the possible outcome. This basic exercise can change the course of your life. (For an additional technique to resolve fear see p. 45.)

Ray's worst fear was that the tax people would catch him. Before the Quest, when he went through some old tax records, he found a huge financial mistake in his favour. He found an enormous amount of funds for which he hadn't paid taxes. He became obsessively concerned and frightened about it. 'Should I tell the taxation department? What if they find the mistake first? Will I be penalised or even prosecuted?' His fear reached epic proportions. During his Quest he did the exercise where he visualised the worst possible scenario. He imagined returning home to find that the tax department had confiscated all his possessions and having to go to jail. Though, of course, this is an exaggerated scenario, Ray struggled in his mind until he found a way that he could accept this outcome. He thought, 'If I end up in prison, I can teach classes to other prisoners on what I have learned about awareness.' In his visualisation he felt good because he was making a difference in so many of the prisoners' lives. When he had finished the exercise, all the fear about his taxes drained out of him and he decided what action to take.

Exercise: Face your Fears

'A fear named is a fear tamed.' List your fears and confront them.

If you are not sure exactly what you are afraid of, take a moment to visualise yourself in a completely vulnerable situation. For each person, this might involve something different. For one it might be physical vulnerability, while for another it might be emotional, intellectual or perhaps spiritual risk. As you visualise the situation that seems to embody vulnerability for you, let your mind float freely to see what the worst threat could be. Imagine the worst possible scenario. This is a way to tap into some of your deepest fears.

If you are not sure how to face or confront fear, one simple exercise is to visualise yourself either overcoming your fear or finding a way in which you could accept the feared outcome. When you imagine overcoming or accepting a fear, it has less power over you.

Death and Old Age

Your body has a limited time on earth. Your body will die. You, of course, will not. There is power in facing the finite nature of the body. Confronting the mortality of your body and facing your death with courage and compassion can allow you to live life more fully. Until you accept your death, it's difficult to truly live. Native Americans have an expression that says, 'Today is a good day to die,' which means that I am complete in this moment. I am ready. I am enough.

We live in a culture that reveres youth and beauty and

denigrates old age and illness. However, all life's stages have value and beauty, even the pain, suffering and ignobility of old age. I still want to experience life in all its richness. Even my tirade against the indignities of age is precious to me. It is all part of the earth plane experience and I want to feel it all while I am here.

Exercise: Facing Death

Your death: imagine going forward to your time of death. Fully confront your death with courage and grace. Grieve if needed. You cannot truly live until you are willing to face your death.

Releasing Attachments

I lived in a Zen monastery for several years and while there developed a deep appreciation for Zen stories. This is one of my favourites. Two Zen monks were walking when they came to a river. On the river bank was a very beautiful young woman who was afraid to cross the river. She asked for help. One of the monks stepped forward, hefted her on to his back, and carried her across the river. He gently put her down on the other side, and continued to walk.

An hour later, the other monk, unable to hold back any longer, burst out, 'How could you dare to carry a woman on your back? You are a monk and a renunciate!'

To which the first monk gently smiled and replied, 'Oh, are you still carrying her? I released her when I put her down on the shore.'

What are you carrying around with you? What are you attached to? Are you attached to your perpetual anger? Are you holding on to an addiction? Are you unduly attached to your possessions? Are you overly cleaving to your children? Are you attached to your beliefs and point of view? Your attachments define and confine you. They can limit the way you experience the world around you.

Some people think that tenaciously holding on to an attachment or point of view is what defines a strong person; however sometimes it's letting go that makes one strong. The opposite of attachment is surrendering, which doesn't necessarily mean that you are giving up anything, or that you are denying your true feelings. In fact when you release your attachment to another person, often the relationship deepens because it is not based on need. Attachment lessens you and non-attachment catapults you in your potential. Surrendering is shifting your perspective to accept yourself and your life in its totality in the moment. It is a natural state of grace.

Exercise: Releasing Attachments

Identify the attachments in your life. Close your eyes. Relax and imagine that there are invisible cords of energy flowing between you and each object of your attachment. Visualise releasing or cutting the cords that bind you to your attachment. Feel the cords drop away.

Step 3: Tapping into the Spirit Power Within

Shape-shifting

There is an energy field that surrounds and penetrates us. It imparts life to all living things. It binds the universe together. During your Quest you can gain awareness of this majestic life force. This is exciting because you begin to see that life is not always as it seems. You can gain an awareness of the awesome and powerful dimensions that lie within you.

You were born into a collective thought form that defines reality in a particular way. Our collective reality agrees that all form is solid and that time is linear. In recent times, scientists are beginning to refute these time-honoured assumptions. Despite this new information, our shared collective reality still defines time as linear and form as solid. However, native cultures throughout the world perceive reality in a very different light. Native wisdom declares that everything, including solid objects, is made of energy in different forms. Shamans throughout history have understood the flexible nature of time and have been able to stretch, condense and even loop time back on itself. In your Quest you can step out of the collective reality and thus out of your personal probability pattern. When you see the world through new eyes you begin to be master of your destiny.

The way to begin to see the world through new eyes is to learn to shape-shift. Shape-shifting means to expand your awareness so you can enter the consciousness of other life forms. It also means shifting your personal parameters so you can sense the energy fields around you. When you've seen the world through the eyes of a butterfly, life expands majestically and nothing looks the same. Looking through the perception of a butterfly, the world is filled with vibrations, colours and shapes that seem unrecognisable and indefinable at first; in fact there is no perception of human beings in a butterfly's reality, aside from movement and colour. A butterfly perceives an entirely different reality from us. How do I know this? I've looked at the world through the eyes of a butterfly.

My teacher, Dancing Feather, a Pueblo Native American, was the most humble and sincere person I have ever known. He didn't speak much but when he did speak, he spoke the truth. He told me that he was in the Fox family. I asked what that meant. He said that he, and his father and grandfather, and his ancestors all turned themselves into foxes to gain wisdom and knowledge of the inner realms. I said, 'Oh, you mean that you imagined that you were foxes?' He looked at me with such patient eyes and said softly, 'No, Denise. We really turn ourselves into foxes.' In that moment I felt truth resonate through his words. Even though it's hard for me to comprehend a human turning into a fox, I knew that Dancing Feather always spoke the truth.

When you begin to shape-shift, you realise that all permutations of life reside within you. This makes a powerful stand for environmentalism because you begin to realise, 'I don't just live on the earth; I am the earth.' When you experience yourself as the earth and the mountains and trees and birds you develop a passion for contributing to the environment.

Exercises: Shape-Shifting

• Learning to shape-shift can allow you to step out of your probability pattern and can open an entirely new dimension to your life. As you sit in your sacred circle on your Quest, look at the environment around you and imagine yourself dissolving and re-forming again to become a tree, a rock, a cloud, a beetle, a flower or whatever is in your immediate environment. Notice how this feels.

• To acclimatise yourself to shape-shifting visualise moulding your body. To do this close your eyes, relax and imagine that you are stepping out of your body. Turn around and see your body in front of you. Reach out with your spirit energy hands and mould the body like clay in a potter's hands. You can either re-form the shape of the body or you can mould your body into another form, such as a stone or an eagle.

I shape-shifted with a seal who was in the bay most of the time. I shape-shifted with the birds and with the sea otters. They chattered as they swam past. I shape-shifted with the trees, the s piders, the cloud people and the stars. I had wanted to see a raccoon. One morning I was sitting waiting for the sun to rise and at the water's edge was a raccoon. Every wish was granted. I was blissful and happy.

Judy Knight, Britain

Sensing Energy

We are constantly immersed in an ocean of energy. The energy that is around us flows and moves in constant, ever-changing currents through time and space. Beneath the surface of fixed objects, existing in a linear river of time, is the reality that energy swirls into form, dissolves and coalesces once again. The world around us and within us is an interplay of these patterns of energy in ever-fluid relationship. Underlying this motion is a cosmic order. When you begin to develop the ability to sense energy, you will discover that all matter has colour and sound. Every plant emanates a shimmering radiant light and at the same time emits a soft hum, unique to its species. Every blade of grass, flower, tree, animal, bird and even every stone emits light and has a unique sound. Some sounds are like low drones and some are like finely tuned hums and some are even somewhat lyrical. To step into the realm of energy, shapeshift into another form and expand your awareness into the realm of light and sound. For example, if you shape-shift into a dandelion, imagine what sound and colours might emit from this plant. Immerse yourself in this awareness. Become the physical, light and sound of the dandelion.

Exercise: Sensing Energy

Relax, close your eyes and imagine that you are in a sacred meadow. Imagine that your awareness expands so that you can sense, see and smell the subtle vibrations within this meadow. Then imagine that you are moving your hand in front of you until you can see a trail of light and sound in your hand's wake as you move it back and forth. You can perceive the ripples of energy flowing through and around it.

Drumming

One of the fastest ways to tap in to your Spirit Power is to drum. From ancient times to the present, people inhabiting every corner of the globe have incorporated the drum into their culture. The drum has the ability to alter consciousness and thus has been used for a variety of purposes, from rousing warriors to accomplish remarkable feats, to being used for healing purposes, to inner mystic voyages. The sound of the drum literally alters brain waves. This has been verified in scientific research. Native Americans call the drum the 'canoe' or the 'horse' because of its ability to allow one to travel to spiritual realms.

Your drum can intensify whatever intention you have for your Vision Quest. For instance, if your intention is to send healing to your family, then your drumming can magnify this intention in a powerful way. If you want to travel inward and explore deep aspects of yourself, then playing the drum close to your heart can alter your consciousness in such a way as to transport you deeply into the inner realms.

On the Quests that I lead, we make drums beforehand and many take their drum into their sacred circle. If you drum while on your Quest, it has the potential to tap you in to your intuition and even connect you to the rhythms of the cosmos. If you decide to take a drum with you, make sure that your drumming won't attract attention as it can disturb your Vision Quest if people gather to hear you drum. If your spot is close to other people, you could tap quietly on the drum with your hand or fingers, which has the advantage of being quiet and yet can assist you to travel into inner realms.

Exercise: Sacred Drumming

Hold your drum close to your chest and allow your awareness to fill the interior of the drum. Rub your hand in a circle around the outer area of the drum to connect more deeply with it. Begin drumming with a double beat. This is an excellent way to start because the two-beat connects us to the heartbeat which is the most primordial sound for human beings. After feeling this sound resound inside you, use whatever beat feels best to you, simply allowing a natural rhythm to evolve. When you stop drumming, close your eyes and focus your awareness on the inner realm within you. This can produce profound results.

Finding your Spirit Name

There is power in your name and it is part of your Spirit Power. Your name is much more than the label that people call you, it is your own unique energy pattern vibration. Used properly, it can open you to spiritual realms and heightened consciousness. It can also be a catalyst for growth, for your name is a direct link to your soul. When you know the name of something or someone, there is a connection between you and that object. In ancient metaphysical traditions people were careful who they told their true name to because it was believed if someone knew your name they could have power over you.

The words we use to describe objects and people have a powerful effect. Companies pay thousands of dollars to come up with names for products that inspire or entice. For example, car names like Bronco and Mustang inspire a rough and ready adventurous individual. Research has shown that a person's name can dramatically affect their personality and the way that others relate to them. For example, someone with a cute or sexy name is less likely to gain job promotion than someone with a more conservative name. But in a much deeper sense, our name defines how we see and feel about ourselves.

In native cultures one had a birth name and then at the time of ascent into adulthood there was a naming ceremony. During the ceremony a name was given that not only was a reflection of the spirit of the person, but was also intended to imbue power into the individual. For example, a child named Eagle Bear would have a definition of self that radiated strength and power. Even in present times in the acting profession names have been changed to give a perceived sense of something grand and exciting, and often career changes follow. In our modern society we do not have a tradition of names of merit. We only have a tradition of birth names, which usually don't reflect our inner spirit. There is value in finding your spiritual name that reflects who you are now, and also strengthens the path of who you are to become in the future.

There is majesty in seeking and finding your name on your Quest. Your spiritual name may come from observing nature and the environment around you. Raven Heart gained her name when she saw a noble raven as she sat in her sacred circle. She said that she felt a deep sense of empathy and communion with the bird and knew that Raven was a part of her true name. Your name may also come in the form of a word or words that don't have a meaning in

English yet have a profound feeling associated with them because of the sound vibration. Ashara's name came to her during a dream while she was on a pilgrimage. She knew it was her true name as soon as she heard it. She said she felt a warm tide of energy surge through her every time she thought of it, even though she had never heard the name before. Your spiritual name can also be made of qualities that define your personal attributes such as the name Strong Heart or Spirit Singer.

The meaning of your spiritual name may unfold for you long after you have received it. Martin searched for his name on his Quest and his attention was drawn to a broken tree that had fallen down. He thought 'Broken Tree, that can't be my name. It doesn't sound very spiritual.' But his inner voice kept whispering the name to him, 'Broken Tree. Broken Tree.' He said, 'Well, Broken Tree it is.' In the months following his Quest, he began to think about his name. In his mind's eye he saw an image of a tree that had broken and fallen across a deep chasm. As he looked he saw that people were able to cross the chasm because of the strength and steadiness of the broken tree. As he reflected on his life he saw that even though he had been broken (he was a recovering alcoholic), through his 'brokenness' he was able to help and have compassion for others. In addition to his work as a solicitor, he worked voluntarily in the prison system to help prisoners overcome their addictions. When he had this realisation, he saw that there was great power and beauty in his name Broken Tree.

When you discover your true name you may choose to keep it secret, only revealed to those close to you, or you may choose to use your name publicly. Either way your spirit name can contribute to personal power.

Exercise: Finding your Spiritual Name

Relax and breathe deeply and fully. Open heart, mind and soul and ask that the Creator send you a name that reflects your spirit. Be open to whatever form your name appears in. Sometimes you have to try your name out for a while to see if it feels right. To do this keep repeating your new name aloud over and over again. Notice how the sound of your name makes you feel. If it is the right name for you, you will feel strongly just by saying it.

Finding your Spirit Animal

The use of spirit animals (called totems, animal allies, or power animals) throughout history is well documented. Native people throughout the world understand the value of connecting with one's power animal. In addition, in some European mystic traditions spirit animals are considered important allies to help one attune to inner strengths. For example, someone working with the fox spirit (called 'fox medicine' in the Native American culture) can develop the ability to become 'invisible' when needed. They can enter and leave a room without being noticed if they choose. Someone working with 'bear medicine' can develop inner strength. There is great value in locating and attuning to your totem animal. In fact, for many people, the discovery of their spirit animal is their single most important experience in their Vision Quest. Connecting to your totem animal not only further deepens your connection to the earth and the creatures of our beautiful planet, but it also begins to bring the qualities that are associated with the animal in to your life.

As a part of your Quest you may want to discover what your animal totems are. Sometimes your spirit animals will appear in your dreams, sometimes an intuitive awareness begins to dawn within you and sometimes they will physically visit you during your Quest.

Catherine, a warm easy-going woman from Middlesex, England, came to the Vision Quest, not because there was a major issue in her life which needed to be resolved, but because she wanted to spend some time away from the pressures of everyday life to deepen her connection to the Creator.

As the start of the Vision Quest approached everybody . . . seemed to get a bit jittery. I began to wonder whether I could spend three days on my own out in the open. I suppose my biggest concern was whether I could go for so long without food. Would I start eating the grass by the end of the first day? Then as we all sat in the Long House on the last evening before the Vision Quest talking about how we felt, a sense of peace and contentment flooded through me. I felt totally resolute and ready for the start . . .

[On the day of the Vision Quest I was intuitively] guided to a beautiful place. There were trees on three sides, but straight ahead . . . looked out over the water to the other islands. It was very calm and peaceful. I spent some time watching a sail boat glide silently out of the gentle mist. A gull floated by very slowly

on a piece of jetsam. I felt an overwhelming sense of acceptance by Great Spirit. I came to know deep in my heart that I am part of the great web of life, that what I do is of value and makes a difference.

Towards the end of the first day I heard a strange knocking sound in the tree above my sacred circle. It was a woodpecker; the first time I had ever seen one! [I felt that] the woodpecker was one of my power animals, not by my choice but because a friend had told me that the woodpecker is the power animal for my birth sign. When I first heard this news I felt disappointed. I would have preferred the mighty eagle rather than the lowly woodpecker, but with time I came to love and accept the woodpecker as my power animal. Woodpeckers drum [with their beaks on trees] mainly to get at their food, but sometimes they drum for the sheer love of it. I love to drum too. It was through hearing the sound of the drum that Great Spirit first called me to the Native American path. The woodpecker above my sacred circle continued to drum away for ages. From time to time the lichen that he was pecking from the branches showered down on to me. A true blessing from Great Spirit. Finally the woodpecker flew away but when I woke up the next morning the first sound I heard was the woodpecker again. This time he did not stay long but he had come to make sure everything was all right. I felt looked after by Great Spirit. The spirit of the woodpecker stays with me always. I have painted the drum I made on the island with a woodpecker design so we always drum together. It helps me to connect back to my sacred circle and the sense of oneness with Great Spirit I felt there.

When I got back to London I felt jet-lagged and I was thrown straight away into the hurly-burly of life and work in the big city. It was as if I had suddenly lost everything I had felt on the island. Slowly the connection with Great Spirit got stronger and deeper again. It endures and has become an essential part of me and my daily life. It always helps in times of stress or uncertainty to connect back to my sacred circle on the island and the deep sense of belonging I felt there.

Patricia Dawson, from Britain, wrote to tell me how she discovered her totem on her Quest.

I was so tired; my life at present is so physically and mentally exhausting that as I lay in my circle I just wanted to sleep. I felt myself relaxing quickly and sleep was close but I was immediately aware of a smallish bear curling up against my back and melting into me. It was actually physically impossible as my back was resting against the hill. I felt no fear and felt no need to turn to look at it. I remember thinking, 'Oh yes, good, it is a bear.' Then I fell asleep.

Exercise: Finding your Spirit Animal

Relax and breathe deeply and fully. Open heart, mind and soul and ask that your animal spirit comes to you. Imagine that you are in a beautiful place in nature. Make it seem as real as you can. Imagine that a dense fog descends on the land. Be aware that your spirit animal is coming to you through the mists. Imagine reaching your hand out into the mists and touching your totem. Notice if you feel fur, feathers, reptilian skin, scales, a shell, a hide or something else. Use your intuition to be aware of what kind of animal you are touching. Gradually the mist rises; imagine talking to your animal ally.

The meanings of your totems are very individual. The specific meanings of spirit animals change from culture to culture but they also vary from person to person. The meaning of a spirit animal will also vary according to the associations the animal has for that person. For example, if a child had a large German Shepherd that acted as a protective guardian then a dog totem might represent protection, loyalty and safety. If another child had a small lively dog then 'dog medicine' might represent the qualities of joyfulness and play. I find one of the best ways to discover the meaning of your power animal is to study its habits in nature. For example in nature bears are creatures of habit. They will often go to an apple grove at the same time every day and will often use the same winter den every year. Hence, people who work with 'bear medicine' are often creatures of habit. There is no totem that is better than any other totem: each has its own power and beauty.

Here are some ways to discover the meaning of your spirit animal after you have returned from your Quest.

- Go on a journey in your imagination and visualise your totem in its natural habitat. Imagine that your totem could talk and ask it what its meaning in your life is.
- Research your totem in nature books. Find out what particular behaviour it has in its environment.
- Imagine yourself becoming your spirit animal and notice what qualities *you* are feeling.
- Research your heritage and find out the meaning your totem animal may have had for your ancestors.
- Research your past lives. The meaning of your totem may come from a reincarnational memory. For example,

in the Orient the crane is connected to longevity but in Celtic mythology the crane is sacred to the ruler of the underworld and is the harbinger of death.

The following listing provides a condensed introduction to the meanings of totems and is by no means a definitive guide, for the realm of totems is both vast and diverse. To do any in-depth recounting of the qualities and special medicine power of each animal would fill several books.

LAND ANIMALS

Antelope: Swiftness, speed, agility

Ape/Monkey: Protection, family, ingenuity

Donkey/Ass: Surefootedness, determination

Badger: Ferocity, courage, tenacity, boldness

Bat: Transformation, primordial darkness, rebirth, initiation

Bear: Healer, strength, stamina, introspection

Beaver: Persistence, group, harmony, productivity

Bison/Buffalo: Abundance, courage, determination

Bull: Strength, stubbornness, determination, power, fecundity

Cat: Independence, cleverness, mystery

Cougar/Mountain Lion: Silent power, self-confidence

Coyote: Cleverness, playfulness, family orientation

Cow: Fertility, contentment

Deer/Stag: Grace, fertility, regeneration, strength

Dog: Loyalty, protection, faithfulness

Elephant: Patience, royalty, power

Elk: Stamina, nobility, warrior spirit

Fox: Camouflage, cunning, quickness

Giraffe: Farsightedness, reaching goals

Goat: Surefootedness, reaching new heights

Hippopotamus: Birth, Great Mother

Horse: Power, freedom, grace

Leopard/Panther: Valour, elusiveness, hidden knowledge

Lion: Self-confidence, radiant power

Moose: Balance, gentleness yet strength, majesty yet awkwardness

Mouse: Discovery, attention to detail, invisibility, scrutiny

Otter: Joy, playfulness, receptivity

Panther: Intuition, inner power

Pig/Boar, Sow: Courage, cunning

Possum: Strategy, stillness

Rabbit/Hare: Fertility, intuition, quick-thinking

Raccoon: Adaptation, creativity, dexterity

Ram/Sheep: Staying in balance in precarious situations

Rat: Cunning, assertiveness, intelligence

Rhinoceros: Ancient wisdom

Skunk: Self-respect, self-confidence, courage

Squirrel: Energy, intelligence, discovery

Weasel: Stealth, cunning

Wolf: Family, loyalty, strength

AQUATIC ANIMALS

Dolphin: Joy, peace, sacred messenger, wisdom

Eel: Grace, power

Fish: Fertility, Christ light, abundance

Octopus: Ancient wisdom

Salmon: Spiritual knowledge, determination

Seal: Grace, joy

Tuna: Ancient power, strength, mobility

Whale: Trust, faith, balance, harmony

WINGED CREATURES

Bat: Sacred mysteries, Great Mother

Blackbird: Mystic ancient wisdom, inner knowledge, mysticism, hidden insights

Bluebird: Joy, confidence, gentleness, modesty,

contentedness

Blue Jay: Courage, speaking one's truth, adaptability

Canary: Sacred sounds, sensitivity, opening of throat charkra

Cardinal: Confidence, vitality

Chickadee/Titmouse: Cheerfulness, joy, enduring, fearlessness

Chicken: Service, sacrifice, fertility

Cock/Rooster: Sexuality, alertness, fertility, enthusiasm

Crane: Longevity, focus, discipline, vigilance

Crow: Magic, mystery, great intelligence, messenger from realm of Spirit

Dove/Pigeon: Peace, feminine energies, maternal instincts, gentleness, love

Duck: Emotional balance, domestic harmony

Eagle: Illumination, spirit, power, creation

Falcon/Kestrel: Speed, grace, power, absolute determination to reach a goal

Goose: Sacred Quests, transformation, mystical journeys, community

Hawk: Visionary, strength, messenger from Spirit, decisiveness

Heron: Dignity, self-reliance, individuality, patience

Hummingbird: Joy, tireless energy, delight, hope

Kingfisher: Peace, prosperity, love, luck

Ostrich: Grounded, balance between ancient wisdom and practicality

Owl: Wisdom, visionary, magic, feminine energies, ancient secrets

Parrot: Optimism, joy, confidence

Peacock: Magnificence, sacred protection, dignity, self-confidence

Pelican: Generosity, self-sacrifice, buoyancy, prosperity

Raven: Messenger from Spirit, ancient mysteries, shape-shifting

Robin: New beginnings, joy, activation of creative inner force, happiness

Seagull: Emotional balance, communication, spiritual messengers

Sparrow/Wren: Cheerfulness, love of home, fertility, boldness

Stork: Fertility, balanced home, new beginnings

Swallow: Daring, freedom, grace

Swan: Transformation, intuition, grace, higher wisdom, inner beauty.

Turkey: Blessings, generosity, service

Vulture: Death and rebirth, prophecy, Great Mother

Woodpecker: Industry, focus, sacred rhythms

AMPHIBIANS AND REPTILES

Chameleon: Adaptation, willingness to change, art of invisibility, sensitivity

Cobra: Royalty, power, wisdom

Crocodile/Alligator: Ancient power, initiation

Frog: Transformation, purification, new beginnings

Lizard: Guardian of the dream time, divination

Snakes: Wisdom, initiation, transformation, creativity, healing

Toad: Prosperity, abundance, Earth Spirit

Turtle/Tortoise: Longevity, stability, home, Mother Earth

SPIDERS AND INSECTS

Ant: Industriousness, stamina, community

Bee: Fertility, abundance, concentration, love

Beetle/Scarab: Metamorphosis, creation, resurrection

Butterfly: Transformation, transmutation, joy, beauty

Dragonfly: Dream messenger, joy, light

Spider: Creativity, fate

MYTHICAL CREATURES

Centaur: Mystical masculine power

Dragon: Immense spiritual power, protection

Griffin: Half-lion/half-eagle: connection between heaven and earth

Pegasus: Spiritual inspiration, grace, holiness

Phoenix: Transformation, rebirth, new beginnings

Satyr: Half-man/half-goat: Nature Spirit, music, dancing, joy

Sphinx: Half-human/half-lion: initiation, Dark Mother

Unicorn: Love, gentleness, strength, purity

Finding your Spirit Song

Often on Vision Quests a personal power song emerges. This is a song that springs forth from your soul. It is not necessarily a song that others will enjoy or that will make the top ten on the music charts. It is a song that carries your power. A power song communicates from your soul and resonates straight from your being. Sometimes these songs come spontaneously from dreams or visions, yet sometimes you have to experiment with the words and the melody. Some power songs have a stanza of words which are repeated over and over again (e.g. 'I am one with the Infinite Sun') but they can also be a ballad that tells your story, your hopes and dreams and visions.

Your song can also come in the form of chanting or toning. A chant can be a sound or sounds that are repeated again and again (e.g. hey ya, hey ya) or it can be the repetition of a word that has power to you (e.g. 'loving'). If you find yourself using a word that is special to you (such as 'joy') when you chant, completely immerse yourself in the meaning as well as the sound of the word. When you do this you are actually bringing the power of that word into your life, and into the world at large. Sound is vibration and the world around us is made of vibration. As you chant merge with your sound and follow the sound into your environment. Notice how the vibration of sound affects and influences the world around you.

When you are chanting, your inhalation connects you to Mother Earth. Your exhalation connects you to Father Sky. Your breath aligns the two opposing yet harmonious forces in the universe: male and female, dark and light, inward and outward. When these two forces are in harmony the planet is in harmony. As you chant you are bringing these two forces into harmony within you and, through you, to the universe.

Exercises: Quest Songs

• Chant your name (either your birth name or your spirit name) over and over again. Ancient mystery schools understood the power of the word. Your name is an energy pattern that connects you to your soul. Repetitive chanting of your name unleashes your soul potential.

• Imagine that you are singing the world into existence. Be creative. Use any sounds that seem to match whatever you are 'singing'.

• Sing your prayers. Create a healing song. Sing a song for healing of others. Sing your soul into the universe.

Finding your Spirit Dance

Sacred dance is prayer in motion. As you are in your sacred circle during your Quest, allow your body to express your feelings through movement. This can contribute to an integration of mind and body. When a child feels an emotion, he expresses it fully both emotionally and physically. Often there will be rhythmic movement at the same time as a child is expressing their emotions. A child can pound on the floor in anger one minute and then jump up and down with glee a minute later. The reason a child can move rapidly from one emotion to another is because they allow emotions and feelings to flow through them. If you are feeling angry, dance your anger. Allow your body to express exactly what you are feeling; this will allow you to move through your anger more quickly.

As adults we are programmed not to show our emotions and we are certainly not expected to express our emotions through movement and dance. So if, in the beginning, it feels strange to stand up in your medicine wheel and start dancing, then start by just swaying back and forth until you get used to the feeling of movement. Let your swaying express what you are feeling. The way emotions can flow through you is to move your body. After you get comfortable with swaying then begin to move your arms, head and legs. Dance your sadness, your sorrow and your pain. Dance your joy. Celebrate your life through dance. Each of us has an unique vibration and rhythm. Your personal rhythm is a sonorous, deep and constant rhythm that defines the essence of you. Of course, your surface rhythms change and flow all the time but your inner rhythm is the same. When you organise your life in harmony with your personal rhythm, life unfolds magically and powerfully. When you are out of harmony with your personal rhythm, there is disharmony in your life.

Exercise: Spirit Dance

Move deep into yourself and imagine that you have found the rhythm of your true essence. Dance that essence. Dance your totem. Dance the environment around you. Dance the earth. Dance the clouds. Dance your past, your present and your future. Dance until instead of being the dancer, you become the dance. Dissolve yourself until the only thing that exists is the dance. Become the movement of the stars in the heavens. Become the rhythm and harmony of the cosmos. Dance through the universe. Dance with abandon and joy . . . and then you will be free.

Several years ago during a Vision Quest I was leading, I climbed up a ridge to check on someone. As I quietly stepped over a steep precipice I felt privileged to witness something extraordinary and wondrous. I watched from a quiet distance as a strong and hearty Norwegian man completely dissolved himself into dance. To describe what I saw and felt doesn't begin to describe the magic of the moment. There was something primordial and powerful in his dance. The movements seemed to transcend time and I felt as if I were witness to some primitive and powerful ritual that gave fertility to the land and a fecund spirit to the people. As he danced, I felt that the doors to life were opening and that the land he danced upon was made holy and sacred through his movements. I sensed a great gathering of spiritual elders surrounding him as he danced in his hallowed circle. I quietly slipped away feeling that I had seen a great wonder. Later, after the Quest, I talked to him about his dancing.

He said that he had been dancing for hours, without stopping to rest, through the night and day, but he felt no fatigue. I believe his dance allowed him to transcend time and space to enter into another dimension where he tapped in to his Spirit Power.

Making a Prayer Stick

Ceremony and ritual have long been a part of the human condition because they allow us to focus our thoughts, dreams and desires into a conscious form. Our inner psyche can pour forth through them and they are a catalyst to bring desire into form. Creating a prayer stick on your Vision Quest can add clarity to your vision and can even change the course of your life. A prayer stick gives tangible form to your prayers. It is an ornamented power object that is created with ceremony and intent. Sometimes the stick is decorated with moss and feathers and shells, sometimes with beads and leather and precious stones, and sometimes coloured yarn is wrapped around it. It is not the method of creation that is important. It is the spirit with which it is made that imbues it with energy. There is great power in the symbolic act of creating a prayer stick. You can use prayer sticks on your Quest for your personal prayers, to chronicle your life, and to help change your life.

Prayer sticks were originally used by Plains Indians for prayers for a hunt, for rain, for planting, or for a loved one. The tribe's survival depended on nature and prayer sticks were thought to be an essential part of aligning with the mysterious forces of Great Spirit. They were originally made in several ways, according to the focus of the prayers, and would vary in size and decoration. For example, a prayer stick for an abundant harvest was made by painting two sticks green with black tips, and tying them together with cording of a specific length. One stick symbolised the male force and the other the female force. Usually the female stick was given a face. A small corn husk bundle containing cornmeal, seeds, pollen and honey was tied to the sticks. Connected to the husk were turkey feathers and herbs. Usually every prayer stick contained a turkey feather because turkey is the 'giveaway' bird, meaning that turkeys sacrifice themselves for the good of all beings, and the feather acted as a reminder that everything you do should be for the good of all beings. The use of prayer sticks has evolved over the years and they are now used in many different ways.

Finding your Stick
The entire process of creating your stick is sacred. It begins with the discovery of your stick before your Quest. To find a stick, go into nature, still your mind and clearly state your intention. You are putting out the 'call' for your stick. Trance Walk to find your stick (see Chapter 3). You will know it is the right stick because there will be something different and special about it. There is great variety in the sticks that are used: small, large, twisted, straight, thick and thin. Some people have used very small twigs and some have used huge sticks that could only be classified as small logs. Once you have found your stick you can Trance Walk to find objects with which you are going to decorate it. You also might want to gather other objects such as pine cones, moss, grasses,

shells, feathers, leaves or twigs to include in the creation of your prayer stick. You can also use coloured string or yarn, beads, paint, pieces of leather or strips of fabric.

A Prayer Stick for Personal Prayers
To create a prayer stick for your prayers, first be very clear what you are praying for. This is essential. Marlin wanted physical healing. He had arthritis that was giving him concern. For his stick he chose a very healthy green flexible stick. He told me he didn't want a stick that was brittle because that was how the arthritis in his body felt. He began the creation of his prayer stick on the second day of his Quest. He began by holding his stick in front of himself saying, 'I dedicate you to excellent health and flexibility in my body and in my life.' Continuing to hold his intention clearly in his mind, he took spring green moss and sky blue yarn which he used for an intricate decoration on his stick. He wanted to create a prayer stick that radiated a feeling of good health and strength. It took many hours to complete. When he looked at his completed prayer stick he said he felt stronger than he had for a long time. You can also make a prayer stick to send prayers to another person or even to a world situation or to an ideal. For example, you could make a prayer stick dedicated to the people of the planet. As you wind the yarn round and round your stick, imagine you are weaving a spirit of love into the world around you.

When you have completed your prayer stick, place it out overnight in a place where the morning sun will touch it. It is said that when the first morning light touches your stick, your prayers go to the Creator.

A Prayer Stick for your Life

You can use your prayer stick as a symbolic representation of your life. To do this, designate one end of the stick as the time of your birth and the beginning of life. Put something in that spot on the stick that symbolises how you view your birth into this life. Then as you work up the stick, mark the major events in your life with different symbolic objects. Once you have completed the stick look at it and see if you feel good about it and it feels like an accurate symbolic representation of your life. Rework it until it seems to convey your life. If there is anything in your life that you are unhappy about you can try reweaving and reworking that aspect of your life. Circling the string round and round is like reweaving the soul.

Gregory had a very dramatic experience at one of my Vision Quests that he felt was helped by the making of his prayer stick. He had come to the Quest to try to heal his very strained relationships with his wife and his two daughters. He decided to create a prayer stick to help improve this aspect of his life. As he decorated his stick he put a black bead on it for him, a red bead for his wife and two yellow beads for his girls. When he had finished, he looked at it and saw that he had placed his black bead a substantial distance away from his family beads. He took his prayer stick apart and rewove it, but this time with the beads closer. When he looked at it it still didn't seem right. All afternoon and into the evening he worked on his prayer stick until he finally felt a sense of union with his family. In a most curious set of circumstances, at the very time that he was reworking his prayer stick, his wife and daughters were discussing the family relationships. They concluded their discussion feeling a great deal of understanding for Gregory. He said when he returned home from the Quest, it was as if a miracle had occurred because instead of strife and discord, there was a wonderful sense of love and community in his family. Gregory felt that he had literally changed his life through the creation of his prayer stick.

Merita Kääntä, a journalist from Sweden, found that the creation of her stick on her Quest helped her unite opposing aspects of herself.

I started making my prayer stick. I had found a small branch with a lump in the bottom that split into two at the end. The lump on my stick represented Mother Earth and the split limb branch represented me in constant battle with myself. I felt [that the split represented the split between my ego and my spirit. It also represented the split between my present and my past]. I decided to weave together my ego and spirit, also my present and my past. So this was what I did. I wove these two parts together with yarn, building a bridge between the two opposing aspects of myself.

Sometimes the creation of a prayer stick can be a catalyst for change as it was for Isja Feenstra, a therapist from the Netherlands.

As soon as I had made my prayer stick, which was a beautiful process, full of learning, I felt myself sliding away. Old stuff, old grief came up. More and more I felt abandoned, and alone. I became sick and cold and cried. At the end, I knew the

*source of my main grief and longing. Then Paulina (one of the
Quest assistants) came. I allowed her in my circle. I felt
nothing. She held me in her arms, and consoled me softly. Very
slowly I could allow the warmth of a human touch to fill me. I
calmed down, left my circle, and greeted a little spider. I had
the feeling that a part of my ego had died. It took time to
recover, but I felt calm, peaceful and loved by the others who
surrounded me.*

When your Quest is complete you can take your prayer
stick home with you as a reminder of your Quest or you can
burn it ceremoniously. In some traditions it is left in nature;
however only do this if everything on your stick is organic
and can decompose easily in nature.

Step 4: Giving Thanks

Thankfulness helps you be receptive to the life force of the
universe. If you don't express your gratitude you lessen your
life force. Being appreciative empowers and strengthens you.
When you call for a vision with gratefulness flowing through
your heart, assistance from the spiritual realm floods into
your being. This is a universal law. If you have been praying
for help and guidance and no one seems to be listening; start
being thankful. Let go of your prayers for what you want,
just immerse yourself in thankfulness for what you have. This
is an act of power. Even if, in the beginning, you have
trouble being thankful, act as if you are thankful. There most
certainly are things in your life for which you are appreciative. Focus your awareness on those things. It is essential to
be in a state of gratitude for wisdom received, for this is the

mystic path to inner truth. When you are thankful, it is inevitable that you will gain in wisdom and inner strength.

An old woman once told me that in Native American tradition one never prayed in order to receive something, one only prayed to give thanks. She said that this concept was central to understanding Native American medicine. I found this idea fascinating. When you focus on what is already good about your life, feelings of neediness and not being good enough tend to fade away into the background. Their urgency seems suddenly less important. Being grateful for what you already have attracts even more good into your life.

Giving Thanks for your Life

If you hold your life in the context of misery and suffering then life becomes a string of difficult events to overcome, but if you hold your life in the context of gratefulness then every experience you have is a gift and offers great value. On your Quest, mentally go through the events in your life and at each milestone stop and allow a feeling of thankfulness to embrace the entire event. Mary did this on her Vision Quest. She had had a difficult life. Her father had abandoned the family when she was seven years old and her mother had become an alcoholic. Often Mary had to take care of her younger brother and sister when her mother was so drunk that she couldn't cope with the responsibility of children. Mary had been in therapy and had worked through many of the deep issues that had arisen from her childhood but still held on to a feeling of deep despair about her traumatic past.

On Mary's Vision Quest, instead of feeling resentment and bitterness, she began to feel thankful for the experiences in her life. She said that usually when she thought of her overall life she felt a sense of sadness fill her. But on her Quest she tried going through her life with the spirit of appreciation. Even though it was hard, as she went through every experience she tried to find something that was good about it. She came to see the events of her life were not without purpose. Every event had a hidden gift for her. Instead of feeling the usual resentment she felt about having to take care of her siblings, she allowed herself to feel thankful for those experiences. When she did this she saw that those experiences allowed her to develop a caring attitude for those less fortunate than her. (Mary is a highly valued nurse who works in hospices.) She said it was such an amazing experience to feel grateful for events that she had resented all her life.

Each of the experiences in your life has been important and valuable and has allowed you to become who you are. When you go through your life feeling thankful, this can begin to transform the way that you see your past and can influence the way that you live your future. There is great power in this, for the spirit of thankfulness can turn a negative situation into a positive one. It can also open your heart to the beauty around you.

Exercises: Being Thankful

• Go through your entire life with the attitude of thankfulness. Feel gratitude for each event in your life, even if you are not sure what you are thankful for. It is never too late to transform your past. A bad childhood is a point of view, it's never too late to have a good childhood. Anything is good if it has value, and being thankful gives value to your life.

• Visualise yourself in a beautiful place in nature. Visualise people who you presently know as well as people you have known in the past, entering into that beautiful place one by one. Allow a feeling of appreciation for each individual to fill you, flowing from your heart to their heart. Imagine stating out loud to each individual why you are thankful for them being in your life. This exercise has the power to transform your life completely.

Giving Thanks for your Body

If you are in need of healing, being thankful for your body can help open the door to healing. Praying for healing sometimes comes from the point of view that your body isn't good. Subconsciously your body hears this and often responds in a negative way. If you radiate love and thankfulness for your body, it often responds by becoming healthier. To understand better how this works, imagine a child whose parent is constantly wishing that their child would stop being so bad. When the child hears these negative comments, they often fulfil their parent's expectations and respond by being 'bad'. However if a parent is appreciative and thankful for their child, the child will often respond in a positive manner. Go through your body part by part with a feeling of thankfulness. Thank your heart, your eyes and your teeth. Thank your immune system. Thank each part of your body. The more parts of your body you thank, the stronger effect it will have on your body.

Giving Thanks for Nature and the Creator

It has been said that when Native Americans first heard of setting only one day aside to worship God they were concerned. They said, 'The Great Mystery is everywhere. All our days are filled with worship of the beauty of God's creation.' When a woman gathering herbs in the forest saw the great span of an eagle's wings silhouetted against the sun, she would pause for a moment with the feeling of worship and thankfulness in her heart. When the hunter saw a massive cedar tree reaching its branches into the sky, he would stop and feel a sense of gratefulness fill him. There was no need to set one day apart, since all days were holy.

Whatever you admire outside yourself will begin to grow within you. For example, if you feel a deep fulfilling gratitude for the old gnarled oak tree that has again and again survived the trials of time, you begin to imbue within yourself the qualities of strength and endurance. Whatever qualities you focus your attention on, in the spirit of gratefulness, will begin to develop within you. Whenever you are thankful to the Creator, the love and energy of the Creator will expand within you. This is a universal law. It's important to remember to give thanks for what you have gained by sharing it with others.

Step 5: Calling for a Vision

Through the simplest alteration of consciousness you can enter into other realms on your Quest. When this occurs, the way of seeing the world around you begins to shift and change. Sometimes reality has an illusory quality to it and time seems to stretch and contract. Things are not always as they seem. At the point when this occurs, you stand ready to embark upon a spiritual awakening, deepen your connection to Spirit, and gain clarity regarding your future direction. It is also during this time that you can heal emotional wounds, and gain compassion and tranquillity. This fifth and last step, 'Calling for a Vision' is covered in the next chapter.

5 *Calling for a Vision*

It is time. You have created your sacred circle. You have prepared yourself mentally and emotionally. You are now ready to call for a vision.

This is an awesome and sacred moment. You stand at a threshold between two worlds. Before you lies a vast new horizon of beauty, mystery and wonder. Behind you lies your past. In the moment that you let go of the cord that connects you to your former life, you step into a realm beyond linear time. Crossing through the mystic gateway may be dramatic and inspiring or it may occur softly like a whispered breeze. However, once you have crossed over you may not go back. Though the form of your outer life may stay the same, your inner life will never be the same.

A vision can take many forms, from a deep insight, to a dream, to a physical manifestation. There are two common ways to call for a vision. One is active and one is passive. Active calling for a vision is called beseeching. This means that you are actively pursuing and asking for a vision. The second way is to be passive and open and wait. There are advantages to each way.

Beseeching

Beseeching means to pray or speak from your heart to the Divine. The words you use are less important than the sincerity of your spirit. You can speak, chant, or sing your prayers. You can call out with your voice loudly and plaintively. You can quietly invoke the Creator without words, directly from your heart. You do not need to be eloquent or explain yourself. Be real. Be honest. Be sincere. To beseech is actively to ask for help and guidance. The best way to call for a vision is to be very focused and yet relaxed at the same time. A chant I use at this time is 'Thy will and my will be one,' so what I receive will be in harmony with the Creator's plan for my life.

Black Elk, a Native American holy man born in the last century, was interviewed in 1947 about his Vision Quest. He talked about staking out a sacred circle for a Vision Quest and then walking back and forth and calling out the traditional cry for a vision, 'O Great Spirit, be merciful to me, that my people may live.'[1] This deeply felt cry to the heavens reminds the vision seeker that their vision is not just for themselves, but for the good of all beings. We are all related. It is important that you are not just beseeching for yourself but for 'all relations'. If you cry for a vision for the benefit of all, the heavens will cascade blessings upon you.

When imploring for a vision, you can call for guidance from the spirit realm to help you. A simple way to do this is to say, 'May the spirit guides, ancestors, allies and angels that have gathered in peace, bring love and guidance. I give thanks for the help that is given, may what is received be for the good of all.'

Spirit guides: Personal guides are often those who have been with you before in other lifetimes and who feel kin-dredship and unconditional love for you. They have been on the earth plane before so they understand the difficulties and challenges of living on the earth and offer valuable support. They are excellent to call upon if you are struggling with earthly issues.

Ancestors: Native cultures honour ancestors and believe that they offer assistance, especially in times of need. It is not uncommon to have your ancestors watching over you on a Quest. They are very good to call, especially if you are dealing with any family issues.

Angels: Angels can bring a message of hope and love, especially on your Quest. They radiate a celestial energy and give love and guidance. It is especially wonderful to call upon angelic energies while calling for a vision. I've heard remarkable stories of angelic encounters on Quests.

Allies: Allies can come in different forms. The most common ally is your totem animal. You can call upon your spirit animal helper to assist you. For example if you need to have an overview of your life you might call upon Eagle Spirit: 'Brother Eagle, help me see my world with your clarity.'

The advantage of beseeching lies in the action. If you are the kind of person who passively waits for opportunities to come your way, and they don't ever come, then taking action might be the best path for you. To manifest your dreams often you need to take action. Go for it. Reach for the stars. If you are having a difficult time on your Quest, beseeching can help you through it. Just keep praying harder and harder until the difficulty eases. The disadvantage of beseeching for a vision might be that you miss a simple and direct message from Spirit because you are so focused on actively beseeching.

Open and Accept

The second way to call for a vision is to still your mind, be open and accept whatever occurs. Transformation and change don't often come in the way that we expect. In fact, it is often because it is *not* as we expected that we can be transformed. Be open. Expect the unexpected. Revel in the unfolding of each new day. Often it is in the quiet moments of life when remarkable insights can occur. Usually, it is not our monumental projects and great plans that define self but the space between these events, the ordinary everyday moments of life, which contain the crucial moments of Spirit that define us. Accept. Receive. Breathe. Observe. Just be. The most common way that visions appear is through intuition, a spontaneous thought or just an inner knowing. Visions don't usually come as a lightning-bolt realisation but rather as a gentle emerging awareness. To encourage your vision, be conscious of the thoughts that float through your mind. Very often, the simple exercise of watching your thoughts can provide remarkable insights into your life and your future.

The advantage of being quiet and open is that you can hear the whispers from Spirit. If you are the kind of person who is constantly on the go and actively pursuing goals, just sitting and being can be an ideal way for you to gain a vision. The disadvantage of being still is that sometimes this means boredom and restlessness. While you are trying to 'be' in the moment, your mind is filling with mental chatter about seemingly unimportant things. When you just sit, you might feel tired and bored and distracted. If you have difficulty ignoring the distractions, just say to yourself, 'And this too.' This simple statement allows you to acknowledge the mental diversion, so you can let it go. What you resist persists, so instead of resisting distractions, simply acknowledge them to let them go. Distractions are a part of your Quest. They can also teach you about yourself. The way you deal with them allows you to gain spiritual power and depth.

The Way that Visions Occur

A vision can occur in many different forms. It can occur quietly, even beyond your conscious recognition, or it can be dramatic and moving. No matter in what form the vision occurs for you, it expands the parameters of your life. It can come through the signs in the natural world around you, your dreams, or even in a manifested physical form. The form is less important than how it affects you. All visions change your life.

Watching the Signs

One of the ways the Creator answers prayers and grants visions is through signs. This is why it is so important to be still to listen and observe everything. Often your vision can come directly from the changes and movements of the nature within your surroundings. When watching for signs, observe the creatures, large and small, around your Quest site. Particularly notice anything that seems unusual. For example, if a bird that is normally timid comes near your site, or if you see an owl in the middle of the day, when owls are usually only active at night, these occurrences may contain hidden meaning. Even ordinary occurrences can be part of your vision. A lone hawk making lazy circles in the sky, an ant tugging something much larger than itself along the dirt, a sudden rise in the wind – all these common events can contain deep meaning for your life.

Watch and listen to the plant life around you. Watch the stars, millions of other planets revolving around their own star-suns, other worlds and other life forms. Even insects near your Quest site can carry special messages for you. Listening to the soft murmurs of the wind, often you can catch a whispered word or hear a personal message. The clouds, especially at sunset, can take on a formation that will carry a sign to you. When you take time really to observe your surrounding environment, you can discover something that uniquely applies to your life.

If you are unsure what the sign means, ask yourself the question, 'If I knew what this sign was telling me what might it be?' Often this can help you decipher the sign. Sometimes the messages and visions that you receive through signs are immediately apparent, but others may take months or even years to unravel. It is often the sign that takes years to comprehend completely that is the most valuable. Your Vision Quest never ends. The visions and messages that you receive through signs go on throughout your life.

Visions appearing in clouds are a very common occurrence. After a recent Quest I sponsored, six different participants came to me to tell me about the great cloud angel they had seen during their Quest. It was amazing to hear their stories. From different parts of the island, and unbeknown to each other, they had all seen the same cloud formation which looked like a large magnificent angel. Though each individual had a different perspective, all were in awe of the grand beauty of this remarkable phenomenon.

Erika Klement, a therapist from Australia, wrote to me about a remarkable vision that appeared to her in the clouds.

By the end of the first day I felt a little hungry but it soon passed. I looked towards the sunset, and the clouds seemed to be shaped like people running to it. It was like being drawn in; back into the beginning of time. The message I heard was, 'We are all going back into Oneness now, no matter what we do or what we feel, we are all going home.' What a wonderful end to the day on which I had asked to receive a vision.

Greg, a sales executive from Texas, watched the pink clouds of sunset shifting and changing form as the sun lowered on the horizon. One cloud formation looked like a phoenix with great vast wings that seemed to dive into another cloud formation that looked like a huge fire. As he watched the 'fire' cloud it seemed to dissolve into an opening flower. Greg felt that it was a powerful message for him. He felt that the phoenix symbolised that he was in the process of transforming into another kind of human being; and his heart was opening like the flower opening to the sun.

Keith Wicks, a British chartered accountant for a Japanese shipping company, told me the following story about his request for signs from the Creator. This experience happened immediately after his Quest during the integration period.

I asked, 'Please show me a sign to prove that I am on the right path.' After about thirty seconds a bat flew into my tipi. Initially shocked, I watched it circle inside, not hitting anything. Several minutes later it eventually found its exit . . . Realising I had asked for a sign, I went to the library in the lodge to look up the symbolism of the bat. Finding the chapter on the bat, it started with the word 'Rebirth' . . . 'Rebirth' was exactly right for me. Most of my friends are now bored silly with me recounting this story, but there were so many more lessons I learned on those ten days of the Vision Quest seminar. Actually, I am still learning from them. The implications to me have yet to find limits.

Renate Nordby, from Norway, watched a slug and a woodpecker which were purveyors of signs which gave her profound insight about her life.

A long slug, unprotected, innocent and soft, made its way across the centre of my circle. I watched that little creature moving; taking its own time to reach its destination. It moved slowly but determinedly. It made its way straight ahead without any rest or hesitation. At the same time, in a neighbouring tree just outside my circle a woodpecker was pecking at a tremendous speed on the bark of the tree. [She noticed that both animals were moving at their own speed and said to herself,] *From today I will act and move in my own speed. By moving at my own speed I can keep in touch with both my intuition and my creativity which give me the strength to keep in focus and be centred and determined . . . I shall love rushing people and respect them for having their own speed. However,*

I shall love and respect myself for my speed and personal rhythm.

When watching the signs to gain a vision observe the symbols that appear to you. Susan L. Schrotenboer, a consultant from Arizona, found her sign was a symbol formed by the trees near her Vision Quest spot. This had a deep and lasting meaning for her.

Two trees grew low on the cliff so that their branches were at eye level when I sat in the centre of my medicine circle. On my right was an evergreen tree that I felt symbolised the eternity of life. On my left was a deciduous tree, symbolising the cycles of life. The branches met in such a way as to form a frame for my view. On the second day of my Vision Quest I sat looking across the channel, watching raindrops dancing on the water and birds swooping for fish. I realised that the frame of branches I was looking through formed a heart. This made me groan because I have always thought that this common symbol for love was trite. Why did this shape appear in my life at that time? From the centre of my circle I looked through a heart and watched the world. I realised that the message was, 'I must turn off the mind chatter and open my heart. I must look at the world with a view from the heart.'

One week after returning from my Vision Quest, I was strolling through an arts and crafts fair. I found a hand-crafted, sterling silver heart-shaped pin that wasn't completely closed at the point. I now wear it as a reminder to keep my heart open. I make sure I wear it when I know I am going to be in a confrontational or negative situation. Learning to live through my heart has changed my thought patterns dramatically and created miracles in how I relate to other people. It has been particularly helpful during job interviews and travelling to new places.

Your vision can come as a direct communication from the signs. In every moment Spirit is whispering to you through signs. Judge nothing. Be open to everything. Watch. Listen. Feel. And signs will unfold around you.

Listening to your Dreams

Your vision can come in your dreams so it's very important to take note of all the dreams you have while on your Quest. If you are not in the habit of remembering your dreams, before you go to sleep repeat over and over to yourself, 'Tonight I remember my dreams, tonight I remember my dreams.' Often this is enough to begin to be aware of your nocturnal journeys. Another dream recall technique is to doodle in your journal immediately on awakening. This can activate the creative, non-linear part of your brain and can bring back recall.

Sometimes dream visions come in a symbolic form which needs to be deciphered. However some dream visions are easily understood and very clear. Herman, a mechanical engineer from Germany, said that his dream vision was extraordinarily clear. In his dream his grandmother, who raised him, was holding him and rocking him while she sat in a large rocking chair outdoors on a clear night. He remembered watching the stars when, suddenly, all of them started to move and form into the letters, 'Open Doors'. He

woke from his dream knowing that his mission in life was to
'Open Doors' for other people. He had practised yoga for a
number of years and was considering teaching yoga. He felt
that his dream was a sign to teach yoga to help open doors
for others.

One woman, who was a property developer for low-
income housing in Africa, had dreams during her Quest that
had a profound effect on her. She dreamed several times of
being an eagle and woke up wondering:

*What did my dreams signify? Why didn't I seem able to get the
message? Groping for some water, I sipped some and looked out
across the ocean to the reddening horizon. All of a sudden I
stared transfixed. There, unmistakably, was a massive eagle
wing of crimson cloud stretched above the dark sleeping island
in the distance. Each feather was etched in brilliant crimson
and gold as the sky brightened. It was so vivid and real but my
dizzy head could not begin to grapple with its significance.
What was this? I asked Great Spirit and my constant spirit
companion to help me understand these signs. Immediately I
saw, with crystal clarity, the head of a proud Native
American, his bronzed features, the feathers about his head
and his red clothing about his shoulders, clear and vivid. Who
are you? You have a message I can't decipher! With that, the
sun burst over the horizon and melted the image.*

*I sat up feeling very unsteady and reached for my notebook,
frantically wanting to take down his message. One of the most
important reasons I had come on the Quest had not yet been
satisfied. I still didn't know the names of any of my guides,
whose daily presence around me I had grown so accustomed to.*

I questioned and wrote, scribbling in a daze as the answers came. 'What is your name?' I heard the name 'Aywa'. 'And what is my name?' I heard the name 'Eagle Feather'. How blind could I be! How much clearer could any message be? Had I once been a Native American then? The deep peace I was feeling was certainly like coming home. 'What have you to tell me?' I asked. I heard the answer, 'You have powerful gifts of healing and compassion. Your ultimate destination is one with all. Accept yourself in your perfect beauty.' My soul was alive with a depth of emotion I had never before experienced, my heart bursting with a warmth that filled my whole being and my circle seemed aglow with a brilliant radiance.

Manifestations

Sometimes a vision manifests in a powerful physical way. In a heightened or altered state of consciousness archetypal images can appear. A large boulder becomes a crouched giant, a tree becomes a sage, a cloud becomes an angel, a twig becomes a serpent. A spiritual name appears. A power song is received. Totem animals materialise. A voice speaks out of the darkness. The unexplained and mysterious occur. Although these aren't normal experiences, the fact that they do happen gives credence to the idea that there are spiritual forces propelling us along our path. Deborah, a therapist from London, had quite a remarkable manifestation experience on her Quest.

During the Vision Quest it became very apparent that my seven-year relationship would have to change, possibly end. The clarity of this realisation was absolute. It felt as if a huge burden had lifted from my shoulders. Until that moment I had not consciously realised how destructive the relationship had become, for both of us. I remember sitting in my circle feeling lighter and more alive than I had ever experienced. It felt like I was at peace with everyone and everything, no separation, no body. I have no idea how long this lasted. It could have been a second or a lifetime. Everything was possible in that moment. I wasn't thinking; just being. It remains beyond the powers of my description.

The next thing I remember is laughing out loud with such a sense of liberation. My mind switched back in and was desperately trying to make sense of it all. It was full of questions and doubts. 'What if? This is a kind of madness, etc.' I focused myself and became aware of the rise and fall of my breath, letting my mind gradually become a little stiller. I tried to watch my thoughts and not get involved with them. I became aware of my surroundings, the sounds and smells, the feel of the moss beneath me. Some birds were calling to each other from the pine trees on either side of me. I focused on their song, it was so beautiful. Just then I saw something flutter right in front of me. A bird flew no more than eighteen inches away from me at eye level. I followed where it went and as it flew towards a nearby tree, another bird joined it.

I wondered if these were the birds I had been listening to, but I didn't have time to think, as they seemed to be putting on a display for me – at least that's how it felt. They flew between two trees, sometimes together, sometimes alone, dipping and calling. It was so natural and simple, but so beautiful, I was full of a sense of wonder and honour for the majesty of nature.

The birds were now both lodged in a tree about four feet away from me. They had been silent and still for a few minutes. I thought that the display had come to an end but my body felt electric and expectant. What happened next is still so vivid, and yet impossible in some ways to describe.

Just as I thought it was over, the birds emerged from the tree, swooping down together, as if synchronised, matching wing beat for wing beat. They were only a couple of inches apart; this in itself looked spectacular. Then I realised they were coming in my direction. It all happened so fast. As they got closer, they pulled apart, still keeping their unity of movement. I stared in disbelief at what happened then, for as they separated, in the space between them grew the most beautiful beaded net! Each end of which was held in either beak. This net was the most beautiful thing I have ever seen. It had a luminosity that shimmered in the light, and at each intersection was a beautiful blue bead a colour between turquoise and lapis. I just stared open-mouthed. The birds circled around me and then flew directly overhead and as they did, they dropped the net over me. I felt its impact as it landed. I started. Blinking, I looked and felt around for the net, but it was nowhere to be seen. It had only taken an instant. I couldn't possibly have fallen asleep. It certainly didn't feel like a dream.

I sat there, unable to take in or explain what I had experienced. I felt washed new. I had been shown the strength and protection that was available to me. I knew that I would have the capability to follow through with the changes that I needed to make in my life. I gave thanks to Spirit for giving me such a beautiful experience. As a result of my Quest I feel a stronger sense connection to all those around me and a greater sense of responsibility for all my actions. The challenges of life are as present as ever, however. I just get out of the hole a little quicker each time.

Linton Pope, a television producer from South Africa, had a very powerful experience where he faced something that was so foreign to his rational mind that it shifted his perception of reality for ever.

I have never encountered a process as powerful as a Vision Quest. Through the years I have studied many philosophies and teachings, and have been through many forms of experimental processes. None has come close to the effect of a Vision Quest.

Upon arriving on the island I was faced with a hurdle – the group of people who had come to do the Quest were not my idea of 'Vision Questers'. During the days [on the island] prior to the actual Quest, buried emotional issues began to surface. I felt out of control! My intellectual process was disintegrating.

The evening arrived to depart on my Quest. It was a very scary yet thrilling feeling. I wanted desperately to begin my solitude but simultaneously wanted to find the nearest canoe and paddle to Seattle. My first night out there was an ego kick. I was Mr Tough, Mr Pioneer. The first day dawned and I felt extreme elation. The first day soon became a little boring and irritating. I found my mind was jumping all over the place. I seriously began to question why I was there.

The second night came and went, mixed with shadows of fear and insecurity. The second day saw everything become more intense, to the point that I was extremely angry and holding back a well of tears. I felt as though I was dying in a sense.

The night soon fell and my emotions seemed to intensify even further. Somewhere in the middle of the night I decided that nothing would stop me and I left my circle. The forests suddenly became dark and intimidating. I cautiously made my way through the woods towards the other side of the island. All of a sudden I heard what sounded like an entire herd of elephants charging through the forest, and they were coming directly at me! I stood transfixed! This was not possible, as the island was small and had only deer and smaller creatures as its inhabitants. The sound grew louder and louder until it was deafening. I ran to a tree and stood with my back to it, hopefully preventing myself from being crushed in the stampede that was now seconds away from flattening me.

I had grown up in the African bush and knew the sounds and dangers of such an event. Suddenly, in a flash, the entire forest became so silent that you could almost hear the stars twinkling. Then a deep male voice boomed my surname, 'Pope'. It was said in a very stern and reprimanding way. My legs almost collapsed. I remember thinking, 'Now you have really flipped out, Linton.' However, I was lucid and anything but delirious. Terrified, yes, but fully awake and aware. After the voice boomed my name the forests fell silent again as though nothing had happened.

I stood paralysed for what felt like an eternity. Who had shouted my name, who was watching me, what in God's name created a stampede out of nothing and then made it vaporise instantly? Did Denise have sound equipment hidden in the trees with scouts watching each person's movements? As paranoid as these thoughts were, they were easier to digest than any other possibilities.

Finally, I made my way back to my circle and entered with a new sense of respect that I was at a loss to explain. Not only was my intellect useless but my mind was now skating on razor blades. Somehow I knew that what I had just experienced was not the result of a clever illusion on the part of any human being. This absolute knowing seemed to shift the perspective of my entire universe.

The dawn approached and I remember praying that this would all end. I wanted out of this place. I hated it with a deep passion. The day was the longest of my life. I drifted in and out of strange states and thoughts. I felt this desperate sense of aloneness that nothing could ever fix. I was truly lost and desperate. In simplistic terminology I wanted my mommy! Images of my mother began to surface, most of which were uncomfortable and irritating. I desperately needed to touch another human being. I spent the rest of the day anticipating my return to the camp. My anger seemed to have shifted into a mixed feeling of love and tolerance.

Sunset and the time to return arrived at last. I gathered my sleeping bag and suddenly I was overcome by a huge sense of loss as I left the circle. I felt as though I was leaving home. I seemed barely able to walk. I felt as though I was gliding across the hill and the further I got from the circle the more the tears began to fall. It felt as though everything seemed to be pouring out from inside me. My body became lighter and lighter. I wanted the walk back to camp to take as long as possible. I was overcome by an intense feeling of freedom, joy and sadness, a state of bliss.

Finally I arrived at the camp to find Janna [another Quest participant]. We sat in silence for a long time, watching the other people drift in from all over. I looked at each one in astonishment. They all had the most beautiful expressions on their faces and seemed to be surrounded by an exceptionally harmonious energy of some kind. Gradually we all hugged each other, and for the first time in my life I looked forward to a hug from another human being. As I hugged each person I could feel their harmony and, most importantly, my own harmony, accompanied by a tremendous sense of peace.

The desire on everyone's part to hug and be hugged was deafening. The most amazing observation was that no one said a word. There was absolutely no need to. What was needed was simply being done, instead of it being spoken about. It was, by far, the most electrifying silence I have ever experienced. It was a very sad goodbye the day we all left; these people were no longer the strangers whom I judged, but intimate souls who had risked their very being, in the name of truth. This creates a bond that lasts for ever!

What if you didn't receive a Vision

One returning Quest participant said, 'Nothing happened on my Vision Quest.' I said, 'Do you mean that you weren't caressed by morning mists, and the night sky wasn't filled with a vast landscape of stars? You didn't hear the lapping of gentle waves against the shore, and the frogs didn't sing at night?' She laughed and said, 'I mean, I didn't have a real vision.' I said, 'If you went on a Vision Quest with an open heart, you had a real vision. Accept your vision in whatever form it came to you, even if it isn't what you expected. Acknowledge it. Honour it and give thanks for what was given.'

Our expectations come out of childhood programming
and preconditioned responses. On your Quest you are embracing a new way of being in the world, where expectations
and old repeating patterns of the past drop away. Growth,
transformation and change do not always fit expectations!

Rich in symbolism, steeped in beauty, everything that
you experience on your Quest is a magical part of your
vision. In ways, perhaps beyond the awareness of your five
senses, seeds are planted in the fertile soil of soul that will
bear fruit in the years to come, even if you have uncertainty
about the form that your vision took. On your Quest you
have appealed to the Creator, to your spirit allies and to
your higher self. Trust that the way that they answered your
prayers was the best way for you. The way to receive a vision
is to accept and surrender to whatever happens on your
Vision Quest. Jaap de Kreek, a former advertising executive
from Holland, said this about his Quest.

*There I was, sitting on the cold earth, watching the pouring
rain covering an empty bay. I prayed for a spark of sun and
thought about the many pleasures of my luxurious life back
home.*

*I waited for the big moment of enlightenment. Nothing
happened. Nothing at all, not even the slightest miracle.*

*Two days were filled with absolutely nothing but silence.
Since I had one day left, I decided to quit trying to call for a
vision. Instead I decided to spend my remaining time simply
enjoying myself. At the time it really didn't feel like a choice .
. . it just happened.*

There and then my life changed!

In that moment, in my circle of stones, my lifelong belief system of needing to struggle and make an effort to achieve success changed. I felt a deep sense of peace fill me. Those days in the beauty of silence brought me to the decision to leave my successful work and to sell my flourishing company. I challenged myself to break through the comforting shields of my daily life, and use my time for growth and adventure.

For me, my Vision Quest was not only a distillation of my fifty-four years of existence but also a turning point in life. In the year since the Quest I have sold my business and I feel free. I can't hide behind my work and my growing success in the world any more. I have much more time to go deeper into myself and now life seems to be an ongoing adventure.

Completing your Quest

Send prayers for others and the planet

No matter what form your Quest took, on a deep level you have amassed spiritual energy. It is extremely valuable to project this energy to others. Complete your Quest by sending prayers, blessings and good thoughts towards people you know and love. Then send prayers to people you don't know and perhaps will never know. Then send prayers to all creatures of our beautiful planet and to the planet, Mother Earth herself.

Clean up

Before you start to take apart your circle, it's important to give thanks to the spirits of that place and to the unseen helpers who gave you guidance. Take time to reinstate the area back to its natural state. Make it look as completely natural as possible. If there is rubbish that is not yours in the surrounding area, take it with you when you leave as a gracious way of giving thanks to the spirit of the place where you had your Quest.

The first hours back

It is very important to be gentle with yourself for the first hours and first days after a Quest. This is a special time when you are making the transition back into everyday life, a time for reflection, integration, grounding and rest. Some people feel ecstatic and exhilarated after a Quest. These responses can mean that the individual isn't quite ready to return to their regular life. They need some time to ground themselves. Some people feel exhausted and for them it's important to rest. Do not complete your Quest and immediately jump back into life. Shorten your Quest rather than shorten the integration time after your Quest, as the integration period is as important as your Quest. Take time to reflect, access and remember what you have experienced.

Sharing with others

Your Quest is not just for yourself. When you return you are carrying sacred energy back for the good of all people. In Native American tradition, immediately after a Quest the initiated individual sat among the elders in council who heard his experience, discussed the meaning of it and accepted him back into the tribe with new status. Often a name was conferred at this time, if one was not received on the Quest.

In the hours immediately after your Quest, be careful with whom you share your experience. Sometimes other people's views can distort your experience and sometimes people can add insight. If you decide to share your experiences, make sure the people you tell are supportive and willing just to listen without adding their interpretation. At times it can be better to keep the insights to yourself. Yet, at other times, sharing increases the value you gain. Trust your intuition on what is appropriate for you.

6 *Vision Quests for Teenagers*

In ancient times Native American children, near the time of puberty, were sent on a Vision Quest as a ceremonial passage into adulthood. Primarily this rite was for boys between the ages of ten and seventeen, but in some tribes girls were allowed to go as well. A Native American Vision Quest was an opportunity for adolescents to seek their spirit guide and their inner strength. Often spiritual guidance would come to them in a dream or a vision, usually in the form of an animal. A typical Quest lasted four days and nights and vision seekers would undergo physical hardships, such as fasting, so the spirits would take pity on them. When the teenager returned to the village with his vision, he was considered an adult. His newfound spirit guide would help him throughout his life, helping him find his path.

Our society is bereft of rites of passage for children, and especially teenagers, as they pass through different stages of their development. The few ceremonies that we have in our society, such as graduation, do not touch the deep spiritual significance that accompanies any transition in life. In present times the Vision Quest offers a powerful way for teenagers to honour their passage into adulthood and to gain clarity to their purpose and destiny. Meadow, my daughter, has been participating in Vision Quests since she was thirteen years old. In the next paragraph, and for the rest of this chapter she shares her own Quest experiences as well as comments of her friends who have also been on Quests. In addition, she gives practical suggestions for any teenager who may wish to embark on this sacred path.

Over the past five years I have been on six Quests in the United States, in places such as Utah, Washington State, and New Hampshire. These Quests ranged in length from one to four days, and my first was in the Cascade Mountains of Washington State. I went with my mother and a group consisting mostly of adults, though there were three other teenagers. I was tremendously excited, but also a little nervous. Looking back, I realise that I did not fully understand the exact meaning of a Quest. When the day finally came, we woke up before dawn and drove in silence to a high vantage point to spend the next twenty-four hours in solitude. We unloaded the vans just as the sun was rising over the horizon, collected our necessary gear, and walked off in different directions in search of our sites. The morning air still cool, our breath left white clouds in the air. While I looked for my 'perfect' site, a voice in my head kept telling me to look for apparitions, ghosts, and the paranormal. To me, a vision had meant a hallucination or a booming voice from above giving me wisdom and telling me my purpose.

I finally found a site on the top of a grassy hill facing Mt Rainier, the highest point in Washington State. I set up camp, made my circle, and sprinkled cornmeal around the periphery to help create a sacred space as my mother had told me to do. In case I couldn't endure the twenty-four hours without food, I saved some of the cornmeal. Once I had finished with all the necessary preparations, I sat in the grass and stared at the mountain in the distance, waiting for my vision to come. I waited and waited. It was very hot so I drank some water and then I waited some more. The sun was pounding on my bare shoulders, so I put on sunblock and then waited some more.

I had read in history books about saints having visions, so I expected a miracle or something special to happen to me too. I didn't understand that a vision didn't have to be anything grandiose. A vision could be a realisation about myself or overcoming my fears. I tried so hard to have an 'amazing experience' that I wasn't sensitive to what I was gaining from spending time alone.

I kept hoping to see something out of the ordinary, like a deer walking over to me and lying in my circle or clouds moving just because I willed them to do so. But the only thing that disturbed the silence was the growling of my stomach. Exasperated, I even began talking out loud.

'I'm still here. Where's my vision?'

'I'm hungry. Where are you, vision?'

'I'm really bored . . . and hungry. I'm not going to wait around for you, vision!'

The hunger grew to the point that it was the only thing on my mind. I remembered the bag of cornmeal I had set aside for an emergency. I retrieved it from my backpack and doused it with water in a vain attempt to make something edible. I set the wet mush on a rock in the sun, trying to make corn chips. I couldn't wait for the mush to dry, I just *had* to eat it. I'll never forget how it tasted. It had the texture of sandpaper and the taste of moist dust, getting stuck in my teeth and in the back of my throat.

Although I kept hoping a vision would still appear, I became so preoccupied with food that I finally left my circle and sneaked into the base camp and took a couple of pieces of barbecued chicken that had been left out. I can't remember any food ever tasting as good. I felt a bit guilty about eating it. However, later my mom said she was still proud of me because I had overcome my natural timidity when I took the chicken. She said that was valuable in itself.

Even though I didn't have the type of vision I expected, nevertheless I gained a great deal from my first Vision Quest experience. When I packed up my site, I felt like I left the young timid Meadow behind and emerged more confident and sure of myself. I was proud of myself for surviving twenty-four hours alone. That was something I had never done before. The other three teenagers in the group were the only adolescents I knew at the time who had ever spent so much time in solitude. It made me feel proud that we had done something that most teenagers never attempt. Since that time I have realised that it's not necessary to have an incredible experience or a vision of the type I had imagined. This realisation has made my other Quests more powerful.

More recently I have done Quests with organisations which specialise in teenage trips. They refer to a Quest as a 'solo' because this word emphasises being solo in nature as opposed to searching for enlightenment or a 'vision'. I think that it would have helped me when I was thirteen to have called my time alone in nature a 'solo' rather than a Vision Quest. While a deeper understanding of self is certainly obtained from a solo, for most teenagers the name solo is less intimidating than Vision Quest. I prefer using the word solo for teenage Quests because it diminishes the stress of having to find a vision.

My longest solo, four days, was part of a semester programme at the Mountain School in Vermont, a boarding
school I attended in my junior year. (The Mountain School
is a school with regular academic classes but also teaches
about nature, organic farming, and animal husbandry.)
During my time there our teachers prepared us for our solo
by teaching us how to bandage wounds in case something
unforeseen happened, how to build a shelter in the event of
bad weather, and how to deal with the inevitable boredom
of being alone in the woods for four days. After much
preparation, forty-five students were taken into the forest
and placed along various woodland streams to spend four
days and three nights.

I spent the four days sitting and thinking. I mostly
thought about things that seemed mundane at the time,
especially considering my surroundings. Most of the time I
felt relaxed and content but I was also worried that my
forty-four friends, also alone in the woods, were gaining the
'secrets of the universe' while I was just sitting.

However, when it was over, I emerged from the woods
feeling a great sense of accomplishment. I had never spent
that much time in complete silence and solitude. It was one
of the most moving experiences I have ever had. In many
respects it gave me a perspective about who I am and my
direction for the rest of my life. The confidence I gained by
knowing I had the courage to be alone in the woods has carried into my entire life. I've generally been shy around peers
and rarely show outward affection. On my solo I realised
how important my friends are to me. I initiate hugs and I
invite people over to my home. I no longer worry that

people don't want to spend time with me. My classmates at the Mountain School had similar experiences. Some gained insight about their life and others learned an appreciation for the land. I have asked my friends to share their experiences with me. The quotes in this chapter are from the journals they took on their solo.

The Importance of Solos for Teenagers

The main events which will have marked my growing up will have been getting my driving licence at sixteen and graduating from high school at eighteen. The next monumental occasion in my life to mark my maturity will be turning twenty-one and being permitted to drink legally. These are not necessarily satisfying or empowering rites of passage. In modern life we do not currently have a traditional teenage rite of passage, a particular point in our life which distinguishes childhood from adulthood. I believe my true rites of passage have been the Quests and solos I have done. I feel more mature after each one because new levels of self-knowledge emerge. These are some reasons why it is valuable for modern teenagers to spend time alone in nature on a solo.

- Learning to be alone with yourself.
- Evaluating your role in society.
- Feeling a sense of independence.
- Gaining inner peace.
- Overcoming your fears.
- Learning the value of solitude.
- Truly experiencing nature.
- Having time away from the clock and commitments.
- Getting to know yourself better.

Learning to be alone with yourself

Most teenagers are not accustomed to being alone. I'm an only child but still I am rarely alone. I'm at school between seven to fourteen hours a day, then I go home to my parents. When I am at home alone, I often fill the silence with the radio, a novel, the television, or telephone conversations. I seldom just sit and think, letting my mind wander.

I think it's important for me (and for teenagers in general) to realise that it's okay to be alone. It's all right to 'space out', stare at a blade of grass, daydream, or whatever else you feel like doing. Abigail Chatfield, a student from the Mountain School, puts it succinctly: 'It's such a strange feeling; not thinking, [just] sitting and spacing out; it's so unproductive.' While some people may feel that just sitting is unproductive, my Native American ancestors sat in stillness in nature 'not thinking' to gain insight and knowledge. It was the art of being alone that enabled those ancient Quests to be powerful turning points in life and eased the individual's integration into tribal life.

Evaluating your Role in Society

Our high school years are a time for us to define who we are and to determine our role in society. A solo is a good time for teens to separate themselves from their community and look at it from the outside with a different perspective. On her Mountain School solo, Allison Cohen questioned how modern teenagers have chosen to live their lives.

I wonder what would happen if I tried to live my life the way I'm living now. Could I do it? Would I ever want to do it? I'm

*doing exactly what I want to do moment by moment. I have
my lemonade, my book and my journal in my bag. Sometimes
I sit and 'be', sometimes I read, sometimes I sing, sometimes I
write in my journal, sometimes I get up and dance around a
little and then sometimes I eat or drink. The only thing which
governs which of those things I do is what I feel like doing. I'm
realising how little time I spent really doing what I want to do.
Most of the time I do what I should be doing and I make myself
believe that it is what I want to do. Maybe they are the same
thing. I really wonder if I could just live each moment as it
comes, as I am now. Would I be happy doing that? Could I survive? Is that really how we're supposed to be living and we've
just messed everything up?*

As a result of this solo, Allison has spent time determin-
ing her priorities in her future life and this has given her a
deeper sense of the role that she will play in society.

Feeling a Sense of Independence

For some teenagers the feeling of independence and accomplishment of being able to survive alone in the wilderness is
as powerful as the actual experience of solo. Sarah writes, 'I
was permitted to go to the Mountain School on condition
that I could not go on solo. I had the biggest fight I have
ever had with my parents about this. I resented their
involvement. Solo was something I really wanted to
experience and they refused. I was finally permitted to go on
solo provided our leaders, Pat and Holly, could see me from
the base camp.' Sarah wrote in her journal at the end of her
solo: 'Looking back I realise what going on solo meant to

me. It meant complete independence.'

For Sarah, solo represented being trusted to make her own decisions and assess a situation on her own. Solo is often the first time a teenager has spent away from home on their own, away from the dictates of others. On solo one does exactly what one feels compelled to do in the moment and that can feel liberating.

Gaining Inner Peace

Ben Pomeroy felt that the solitude in nature on solo allowed him a deeper sense of peace. In his journal he wrote:

For the past few days I have been living a simple and enjoyable life. Waking up with the sun, making strong tea and eating cheese and bread for breakfast. My day is dictated by my hunger, sleeping desires and inclinations. Nothing much has worried me, except an occasional rain cloud. I have reached a level of calmness and peace. Quite simple activities, like reading or drawing by the stream, are most enjoyable to me right now. Gone are the bright lights and loud noises, sharp edges and foul smells. Here is a world of perfection and simplicity, where one may just sit and observe the soft beauty of his surroundings to achieve happiness. I feel like I am a Buddhist monk on a mission of revelation or a young Indian boy on a Vision Quest. I am alone in nature with my basic necessities, nothing more. I have left the distractions and temptations of civilisation to return to where I might find peace, harmony and a balance between myself and nature. It is possible to co-exist harmoniously with the natural world, if one is wise and respectful.

When doing a solo, teenagers usually focus on keeping warm, remaining hydrated, feeding their stomachs (if they choose to eat), and releasing the wealth of thoughts that they've been storing in their minds.

Usually the anxiety about school or the English paper they should write, the calculus assignment that is due, or the impending college applications, all drift away. The things that usually fill their minds at home seem very far away. They realise that most of the things that they are usually concerned about are not really very important. Of course when they get off solo, they will probably have to write the paper, do the maths, and fill out the application, but those tasks seem easier after solo. There are very few things that we absolutely have to do in life . . . eat, hydrate, and stay warm. Because of my solo experiences, I have a more relaxed perspective on my life.

Overcoming your Fears

The thought of spending hours alone in the woods can elicit a number of fears, many of which are conquered by the completion of solo. Going out alone into the woods is an excellent way to face these fears and overcome them. For most teenagers the biggest fear is being alone. I believe that this is because as children our definition of self always comes from other people. Solo offers an opportunity to find out who you are without the definition from others.

Jessica Taverna explained her fear when she realised she was completely alone.

I was putting any words I could think of on to the pages, anything to stave away NOTHING. As I wrote, my heart pounded, blood pulsed through my veins and my hands shook, making it hard to grasp the pen. Fear was creeping into every bone and muscle in my body, into every inch of my soul as the words became scarce, the thoughts refusing to flow. This fear was strange, deeper than any I had ever felt. It went beyond worries about my tarp and my food.

It was fear of being alone with myself. Solitary, just me, nothing that had to be done, nothing to distract my mind from me. All the time in the world to think about myself. Within a couple of hours from the start of my solo, I knew the basic premise of what the next few days would hold. With only nature, myself, and a journal filled with stark white pages begging to be covered in words, I would be forced to confront the only person I had ever shied away from – ME. This extended period of solitude offered me the opportunity to contemplate my interior self, what controlled my instinctual reactions to things, the virgin me, pure, unadulterated by the dictates of society. This was the part of myself that I hid, both from others, and often from myself, the part of sadness and jealousy and hidden passions and insecurity and desire.

Though Jessica went into her solo afraid of being alone and fearful of what she would find within herself, she finished it with a deep feeling of accomplishment. She pushed through the fear and found her hidden self. If she hadn't had the fear, she might never have realised that there was part of herself that she had hidden from herself and from others.

Teenagers who live in cities, like my friend Allison from New York City, who often have not spent much time in the wilderness are usually particularly afraid of being alone. For these city teenagers being alone at night in the woods can be quite frightening. Allison told me before she went out on her solo that she is more afraid of being alone in the woods than she is out alone in New York City. She said that in New York you are most fearful when you are alone because then you are more likely to be mugged or approached by a stranger. She is safest on the streets when there are many people around. During her solo she felt that she overcame her fear of being alone and now she feels very comfortable in the woods and being by herself, though she is still cautious in New York City. She said that she now sits alone among the trees or in a vegetable garden and just enjoys being by herself in the company of plants.

Gwyn Welles, a Mountain School student also from Manhattan, is like most teenagers. She is rarely alone. She constantly surrounds herself with others. She went off into the woods for her four-day solo wondering what she would do without a companion. Of this experience she says:

I was uncertain about how I was going to spend four days alone. I was nervous about seventy-two hours of no conversation except for the little voices that consult in my head. I did not question my survival; I had plenty of clothing and enough food to open a roadside stand. I did not fear being eaten by a bear; New Hampshire is not bear country. Survival of body I was certain of, tranquillity of mind I was not. I had never spent more than a day alone. Even then, it had been in the comfort of my own home. I realised, as we approached my solo site, that solitude was a companion I did not know very well.

There is enormous power in a teenager realising that they can overcome fear. Even overcoming one small fear on a solo can be a valuable step in learning how to overcome other fears that will occur later in life.

Learning the Value of Solitude

As Gwyn overcame the initial fear of being alone, she realised that she could actually enjoy the solitude.

I have been with myself my entire life. So why was solitude a foreign state to me? I realised, as I took off my backpack and sat down . . . I rarely had been with myself. I did not know solitude because I had always avoided it. At age six, I was first to arrive at the birthday parties, eager to play musical chairs. At sixteen, I for ever was ready to gather a group for a game of Pictionary. On reflection, it is clear that I went to great lengths to guarantee that I was not alone. Being alone was awkward. If one is alone it is not out of choice, it is a result of rejection and denial. I remember when I was younger, sitting alone in my room and thinking to myself, 'What is wrong with me?' I was unable to be happy when I was alone because I believed that I should have been somewhere else. To be alone was not important. To be alone was not natural.

At seventeen, I was finally encouraged to [go on solo and] be with myself. At this moment, to be alone was natural; to be alone was normal; to be alone was the only thing I could do. Perhaps I questioned solo less than other solitary experiences because I knew that forty-four other people were alone in the woods drinking iodised stream water and sleeping under the stars, but for the first time I allowed myself to look beyond the prologue of my situation, solitude, and I was able to discover the plot. I decided not to take many things out of my backpack. My novels remained resting under my sketch book. Instead, I took thoughts out of boxes whose locks never knew that keys existed. Alone, without distraction, I was able to think about nothing but myself. I discovered that to be alone is not to be lonely; it is not selfish, but truly liberating.

Truly Experiencing Nature

Many of us get caught up in our busy lives and we forget to take time to appreciate the earth, the land which sustains us. Nature is an integral part of our lives, the trees create the air we breathe, the rivers and lakes supply us with water, the plants nourish us and the animals we eat. Even those of us who spend quite a bit of time in nature hiking and camping often do not truly see nature. When I'm hiking, instead of experiencing the beauty of nature, I find that I spend the majority of my time staring at the ground to keep from tripping. The subtle sounds of the wilderness are masked by my talking to my hiking companions.

One of the only times that I can truly appreciate the natural world is when I'm on solo. Solo gives me the opportunity to study moss growing on a rock and the patterns leaves make after they have fallen to the ground. Ben examined his solo site quite closely and wrote about his discoveries in his journal.

The day is winding down and sun has begun its descent behind the mountains. A soft warm tone of yellow splashes through the forest. The kind of light only found in the late afternoon, when day is coming to a close, but allows us a few more hours of play before sunset. Maybe the clouds will be considerate and let me see sunset. These past few days have been a guessing game with sunshine or rain. Groton Forest seems to be a place that Mother Nature intended to be wild. These woods were once farmland. Old stone walls reveal boundaries of the past. They are now covered up by moss and overgrowth. Nature seems to mock the idea of property rights. Old apple trees in a meadow tell us of what is grown. The apple trees are now wild again, rejoining their counterparts as another piece of this mosaic aboretum. The meadow is overgrown and wild. Grass and weeds and wildflowers mingle together without fear of the farmer's tractor. What drove away these farmers? Did the poor soil of these hills save the woods?

When Sarah was finally allowed to do solo, she questioned how our society has veered away from all that is natural.

Even in this attempt to be in nature and of nature, I am constantly reminded how far removed I am. Looking at myself right now, sitting in a plastic shelter with a plastic groundsheet in my Crazy Creek chair and synthetic sleeping bag, cold, in my layers of polypro, wool and fleece, is this really the closest I can get to nature? What does that say about my culture? We perceive ourselves as above nature, superior and controlling. Yet I can't survive alone in nature without carrying in my

pack filled with food and warmth. I can't even drink the water
without putting chemicals in it.

I believe that it is important for teenagers to be able to
have the opportunity to spend time alone in nature. Perhaps
if all young people did so and listened to the heartbeat of
the land, our society would be more peaceful and attuned
to our natural resources.

Having time away from the clock and commitments

Many teenagers live according to the clock and according to
what others tell them to do. At school we have less control
over our time than we will in any other part of our life. We
are required by law to go to school from eight in the morning until three in the afternoon, then we are asked to go
home and spend a number of hours on homework (at my
school the average is three hours a night). Sports practices,
play rehearsals and band practice are just a few of the commitments that fill our time. We still live at home, so we are
expected to attend family functions and help around the
house. There just isn't much time left in the day once all
those things are done.

When I first started junior high school, my day was completely dictated by my watch. I timed my morning to the
minute. I had fifteen minutes in the bathroom to shower
and brush my teeth, fifteen minutes to get dressed and
arrange my book bag for the day, and fifteen minutes to prepare and eat breakfast. If for some reason I got ahead of
schedule, I would use the remaining minutes to comb my
hair or put a ribbon in it or something. I left the house at

precisely 7.04 a.m. to catch the bus. I became so obsessed with time my watch was a constant source of stress for me. I finally had to get rid of the watch in order to keep myself sane. Remarkably, I rarely missed the bus after relinquishing my watch. That was seven years ago and I haven't worn a watch since.

Justin Monroe was also accustomed to his watch telling him where to be and when to be there. He didn't take his watch on solo. He realised that he was finally free from the confines of time which normally ruled his everyday life. He said it was a relief to take off his watch and not worry about the time. During his solo he said:

Out of habit I still wanted to look at my watch because I thought that I should be doing something constructive or meaningful with my time but as I watched a stream that ran by my campsite I found that for the first time in my life I truly was at peace in nature. I began to know the land. The frog pond behind my campsite became silent whenever an animal came towards the pond. I have since begun really to listen to what's around me.

Getting to know yourself better

One spends many hours on solo just thinking. Besides the physical landscape around your site, there isn't much to think about except yourself. Solo is a time to question who you are and who you want to be. Through journal writing and intense thinking teenagers often return from solo with a deeper understanding of self. There isn't anyone or anything to distract you. Your only entertainment is yourself.

I've been amazed by the things that I have learned about myself from solo.

Ben became more deeply acquainted with himself through his awareness of intricacies in nature he didn't usually notice in his normal life.

I sit here writing under my tarp with the patter of rain and the chirping of woodland creatures to set the ambience. The air is crisp and cool and my bones are chilled. I bundle to stay warm and write with a fingerless glove. For the first time in a long time, I realise what I am: a human, an animal, a living organism. I am aware of my heartbeat and my breathing. I am aware that I am alive. I am aware that I will die. I have temporarily stopped and examined myself and what I am doing. I am existing and performing life functions. My body is constantly pumping out thoughts, criticism, anger and love and revelation. I am not merely Ben Pomeroy playing out some role or purpose. I am an organism fighting, creating, and loving in order to both survive and enjoy life.

Often this kind of self-knowledge can come from stream-of-consciousness journal writing. Writing whatever comes into my mind, without stopping to think, without lifting the pen from the page, and without stopping to worry about punctuation can allow for remarkable self-discovery.

Jessica tried this stream-of-consciousness technique in her journal and felt she got to know herself much better.

I began to look back over what had been produced during the past twenty-four hours. [In my journal] I discovered that I had written over thirty pages. As I flipped back to a blank page to begin another marathon of words, something from the previous evening's writing caught my eye. I paused to read. As previously I had not been able to stop myself from writing, I now found that I could not stop myself from reading. I was caught up in the web of my own words, seeing them as if for the first time. I only vaguely remembered having written them. Certain individual words and phrases were distinctly mine. There were some thoughts I could conceive of having. But as a whole the writing was unfamiliar. As I read and reread the thirty pages, I found hidden within the trivial lists and mumbling an insight into myself which I had never experienced. This writing seemed more honest, less contrived, than any I had ever done, even in previous journal entries.

I found many things in that writing. I found that I had a capacity for personal expression I had never seen before. I found a bitterness over certain disadvantages in my life that I barely acknowledged as disadvantages. I found a passionate love for the squirrel that scurried along the stream, for the pines that lined the banks, and for the moss-covered rock that was my seat. I found secret desires I did not know existed. Clues to my inner self could be found in the connection I made between topics, in the particular words I chose, even in the varying size and legibility of my handwriting.

Frequently Asked Questions by Teenagers

Many of the general questions about Vision Quests are covered in Chapter 2. The questions below are often asked particularly by teenagers.

How can I do a solo?

The safest and easiest way to do a solo is to go with an organisation that is trained in taking teenagers on solos. Some high schools have solo programmes as does Outward Bound. There are also many groups that take adults on Vision Quests which are slightly stricter than the teenage solos I have described, but many of them would welcome teenagers on their trips.

If it is not possible to go with an organisation, you can plan your own trip. For safety, I would strongly urge you to go with a group of friends. Get a group of about three to ten friends together with at least one responsible adult and choose an area where you probably won't run into many other people. For instance, I wouldn't do a solo in a park or any place in nature that is often frequented by tourists. Good locations are Wilderness Areas or National Forests. Visit the area before you go out on solo and pick your sites. Make sure you can find them again.

Last spring I spent three weeks hiking in the canyons of Utah in a Primitive Area with six friends. We hired two adults, trained in taking teenagers into the wilderness, to come with us to ensure our safety. After we had hiked for two weeks we prepared for a twenty-four-hour solo. Our leaders scouted the area and found a suitable site for each of us. Mine was on a rock ledge above the canyon floor. I had a view up and down the length of the canyon. Periodically our leaders checked on us. If we needed anything or had any problems, we could signal them over to our site and ask for help. It was comforting knowing that they were there.

It is important that a responsible adult, versed in outdoor

survival, goes with your group. Take them with you when you pick out your site so they know exactly where you are. They should set up a base camp and they should be there at all times during your solo in case anyone in your group needs them. Every member should know the precise location of the base camp. When you go out on solo, the supervising adults should check on you at least twice a day. If you do not wish to see them, devise a system where you raise a flag in a designated spot each morning and each night and they will lower it each time they come. If the flat is not raised, they will know that something may be wrong. You can also leave paper and pen at the flag for writing notes to the person checking on you. This is especially helpful if it rains and your clothes or sleeping bag get wet or if you need more water or food. You may also want to update them on your emotional well-being.

How do you pick a place for your solo site?
When you pick your site, keep in mind that you should be near enough to your friends so that they can hear you if you shout or blow a whistle, but not so close that you can see each other. You should not break someone else's solo because you are bored, scared of things such as the dark or being alone, or if you can't stand the solitude. Though you may want to be far away from your friends, I can assure you that you will feel safer knowing you can reach them if necessary. *For your own safety, you must do solo with friends nearby.*

If you are doing an extended solo of approximately four days, it is especially helpful to be near a lake or a stream. Take iodine pills or a water filter to treat all your water as much of the water in the wilderness has bacteria which can make you quite sick. Properly treated water will be safe to drink. If you carry in your water, you need to bring plenty. You should drink approximately four litres a day, though this varies for every person and the air temperature. Even though you will not be doing anything physical on solo, it is still vital that you drink enough water.

Pick a site where you will be comfortable for an extended period of time. For some this is high on a hill where you can look out at a view and feel uplifted, and for others it is being nestled within the trees. Be sure to find a flat place where you can sleep. A comfortable night's sleep will add to your over-all enjoyment of your time alone in nature. The most important thing is to find somewhere that makes you really happy.

How do you pack for a solo?

Pack appropriate clothes for the weather. Even if the weather forecast indicates pleasant conditions while you are on solo, bring warm clothes. Weather can change in an instant. You won't be doing anything active, so it will take quite a bit more to keep your body warm. Take a closed-cell foam pad or Therma-Rest and a warm sleeping bag, preferably one you have used before so you know it will keep you warm. You may want to take a tarp and rope to build yourself a shelter in case of foul weather. You should definitely take a small first-aid kit, filled with plasters, first-aid cream, and a woman's sanitary towel (this works remarkably well in absorbing blood if you get a deep cut). Though I haven't heard of anyone having any problems on a solo, it's always a good idea to be prepared.

Items you may also want to take: a journal and pen, a book, a flashlight, watercolours, musical instrument, food, and toilet paper (carry this back out with you in a bag so you don't spoil the environment).

Can I take a book to read?

I have done solos with and without books. Many 'hard-core' solo leaders would frown upon taking reading material because it removes you from your immediate surroundings. Although books can quite easily transport you away from the experience, certain books can help you better understand the land around you. On my solo in the canyons of Utah I spent twenty-four hours perched high on a ledge looking down into the canyon below and up at the canyon walls above me. Anasazi ruins, pictographs and petroglyphs decorated the canyon. On this solo I chose to read *Desert Solitaire* by Edward Abbey, and his descriptions of the canyon country gave me a deeper understanding of the area. My only suggestion in choosing a book is not to take any sort of reading that you *have* to do or *should* do. This would include books for school and college preparation guides (I actually know a teenager who took college test vocabulary words with her to study). Take a book that will inspire you spiritually or connect you more profoundly to the land.

Will I get better results if I fast?

No, not necessarily. Some teenagers choose to fast on solo, following the traditional way of Native Americans. Others choose to take food. The Native Americans fasted so the spirits would take pity on them and come to them in a vision. I believe both ways lead to results. I have done the majority of my solos with food. If I don't have it with me, I become infatuated with it. It's all I can think about. Most teenagers are still growing so I think it's important to take food. The solo I just completed in Utah was the first time I didn't have anything to eat. I would like to say that solo was more powerful because I fasted, but I honestly didn't notice any other difference.

The traditional reason for going without food is to cleanse your body and to keep you from getting too caught up in the preparing and eating of the food. If you think you want to do a solo without food, I would suggest taking it with you all the same, intending not to eat it. I have a friend who took all the food with him that the Mountain School told him to, but he didn't eat any of it. Christina Capone also took all the prescribed food with her, but with the intention of eating it. On her solo she found that she wasn't very hungry. She returned from the woods after her four-day solo with her food bag full, having eaten only her chocolate bars and apples.

Everyone's body is different and only you know if you can fast on solo comfortably. If you choose to fast on a lengthy solo, I would suggest doing a practice run in the comfort of your own home. Try fasting from morning until evening and see how you feel. If you have any question about your comfort, take some food with you. You do not have to eat it. Most importantly, remember that you do not need to be an ascetic to attain results.

How far should I be from other people?

If you do a solo with an organisation or a group, they will place you a certain distance apart from others. In most cases this is at least a hundred yards apart or within hearing distance of a whistle, but out of sight of each other. If you are creating your own Quest, before the solo begins sit in your circle and yell to make sure that the others can hear you.

What if someone does come near my site and starts talking to me?

The best thing to do if this happens is to explain what you are doing. They will most likely respect your desire for privacy and will leave you alone.

Should I take a journal?

Journal writing can be a great way to unleash the thoughts and feelings in your head and leave you with a lasting memento of your solo, though like a book, journal writing can distance you from your surroundings. When writing one can become oblivious to the weather and the landscape. There is also a tendency to analyse too much and to think too much. In a solo entry of mine, I wrote vigorously for a number of pages, then I ended the entry by saying: 'I feel like I'm analysing this experience far too much already and it's only the first hour or so.'

In her journal, Jessica released feelings through vigorous writing.

I awoke at dawn, momentarily perplexed by my surroundings. After pausing for a few moments to get reacquainted with my forest home, [I thought I would write] until I was completely calm . . . The words just continued to flow. It seemed that I could not stop myself; I wrote without effort, without pausing to think. For the next two days, I continued to write to fend off lingering fears, loneliness and tears. Putting a continuous stream of words on paper made me calm during those four days, and has ever since. Those words allowed me to look into my soul, to see the person that existed away from society and its constraints. Via words, I survived solo and gained insight into who I am.

Is it okay to walk around my solo site?

It's okay to walk around a bit. You will certainly need to walk to the stream or lake if you do not bring water with you. You will also want to be far from your site when defacating (see Chapter 2). However I would suggest not exploring too far from your site. The main reason for this is safety, but also staying in one place encourages careful examination of your immediate surroundings and a sharp focus on your thoughts without distractions.

What is a good age to go on my first solo?

The age that a child does their first solo completely depends on the individual. I don't believe I could have handled a lengthy solo before the age of thirteen. The majority of teenagers I know who have done solo are about sixteen or seventeen, which is a good age because you are old enough to deal with the fear and the boredom, but still shaping and defining who you want to be. This time alone is a great way to focus on yourself and identify the parts of your character that you want to accentuate in your future.

Younger children can do an abridged version of solo by sitting in the garden for a few hours alone. I know a mother who created a sacred circle in her back garden for her ten-year-old daughter to do a four-hour solo. The mother stayed nearby to make sure the experience was enjoyable for her child and the young girl was completely ecstatic afterwards. I believe that you can get just as many results from a short solo as from a long solo. Your intention is much more important than the time you spend. One time I sat in a hay-field for an hour, wrote in my journal and gained as much of a clear sense of my direction as I got from the four-day solo. (However it's fair to say that the time spent on my solos and Quests may have prepared me for that special hour.)

Is it okay to bring materials to remember the location such as a camera, paints, pens, etc.?
Solo is a time to live with the bare necessities, to live deliberately, so it's best to leave all modern devices at home. However, I think paints are a great way to study the landscape and have something to remember it by when you return to your normal life. I don't suggest taking a camera, though. If I have my camera with me I have difficulty immersing myself in nature. Rather, I see nature in terms of photography textures, patterns, shapes, and shades of grey. The stream, the rain, the woodland creatures all become subjects and I forget that I can learn about myself from these things. If you really want a photograph of your solo site, take a camera with you when you first go out to scout for your site before you actually go out on solo.

What if I get lonely, bored, or scared?
You may encounter all three of these things, but that is all

part of the experience. You will grow from pushing through the loneliness, moving to the state beyond boredom, and facing your fears. If the loneliness, the boredom, or the fear get to be too much, or if you just aren't enjoying yourself, you have the right at any time to break your solo. It's not a sign of weakness or lack of courage to break solo. You can do it at any time. If you do go with a group of other teenagers, please remember that you cannot break anyone else's solo. No matter how bored you get, you cannot enter someone else's site and disturb their solitude.

What if my solo doesn't feel enlightening or life-changing?

Solo can be many things for different people. Sometimes solo experiences will allow you to realise things about yourself and make decisions that will entirely change your life. But solo is not always an incredible experience. Often solo can be just a pleasant and restful way to spend a few days. When going into a solo, it's best not to think that this is the one and only time that you will do this – that puts unnecessary pressure on you for it to be an amazing experience. You can do as many solos in your lifetime as you wish. They will all be different.

Can spending time on a solo help me with a problem or life direction?

If you go into a solo with the intention of answering a question or solving a problem, you may find some answers. Sometimes you have to search for answers and wait for signs and other times they come to you 'clear as day'.

When I was on my four-day solo in New Hampshire I spent a great deal of time thinking. I went on this solo without my journal, a book, or paints. I spent seventy-two hours sitting beside my makeshift tarp shelter, beneath the canopy of hardwood trees, just thinking. I thought about a great many things in those seventy-two hours. One of the main things that kept coming to my mind was love. I thought about my friends with boyfriends and wondered when it would be my turn. In the few weeks prior to solo, many couples had started to form around school. I sat in my solo site and counted six new couples out of the forty-five students in the school. I couldn't figure it out. Why had love never happened to me? I was seventeen and tired of waiting. I stared at a small shrub with a solitary dead leaf hanging from its branches. I asked nature to give me a sign that love was in my near future. If the answer was yes, I expected this leaf to fall from the branch. I thought this was a good set-up because it was sure to fall soon anyway. Just as I made this deal with the power of nature, I heard a raucous noise behind me. I turned my head to see what was happening. There were two squirrels mating in the tree behind me, chasing each other up and down the trunk and across the branches. I thought this was a good sign.

Someone once asked me why I had been on so many solos. I told him that I love having the time to be by myself in nature to think and just to 'be', without the constraints of time. A solo gives me a sense of peace, a chance to know myself a little better and to feel independent from others. The values I've learned and the knowledge I've gained on solo have been invaluable. I can take what I have learned on solo and apply it to the rest of my life. I wish all teenagers could have this opportunity.

7 Integrating your Quest into your Life

There is usually an adjustment period after any kind of Quest, whether it is an extended Quest in nature or a pilgrimage or a Vision Walk. It's valuable to comprehend some of the transitions that may occur as you incorporate your vision into your life. It is also useful to gain understanding of some of the potential pitfalls, as well as how to avoid them, so your integration period is easy and joyous.

The most usual comment I receive from people in the months and years after a Quest is that they feel a much deeper communion with loved ones and they also often experience a depth of universal love for all beings. Rick Mauricio, a lighting engineer from Britain, shared these sentiments with me about how his relationships changed as a result of his Quest.

It's been almost three years since my Vision Quest. As a result of my Quest I find that I have deeper relations with everyone I meet and I know they feel the same. There is a 'connectedness' which pervades every encounter. I find that even when I pass people on the street, particularly children, they often change from being angry to gleeful. They seem to mirror what they feel from me, which is generally joy.

I've discovered that being myself is my truth. I've found the Me that was always there and I've understood some of the reasons behind who I am. One of the most profound realisations I've had is that being who I am is enough.

Personal relationships have also changed for me in a positive way. I now understand the many aspects of love . . . and I understand that giving and receiving are much the same thing. I understand the camaraderie felt by men for men that goes beyond words or actions. Souls touching souls. I also know that a woman, who is one's partner, must feel that she is special, even while the man [that she is with] is feeling unconditional love for everyone and everything. I know this seems a simple thing to understand but I have been incredibly slow in matters of the heart.

After a Vision Quest or a pilgrimage the world is the same, and yet very different. For most, life no longer seems random and arbitrary. Seemingly unrelated events begin to take on meaning and offer signs and personal messages. The messages were always there but now one becomes aware of them and the desire to follow them can become very strong. This is fine if the changes that are made are in harmony with conventional life. However, the challenge comes when society, friends and family feel that you are supposed to embark on a certain path of action, even though your vision points you in another direction.

When you begin to grow spiritually, sometimes the people who are closest to you are threatened by that change. Part of their definition of self depends on the relationship patterns that have developed between you and them. When you change it can potentially threaten the personality dynamics of everyone who is in close relationship with you because they may feel that they have to change as well. However, although there is an adjustment period after return from a Vision Quest, usually after a settling-in period others see the power and beauty of the change and everyone benefits. A spouse or child or parent of a Quester will often come to my Vision Quest the following year because of the improvement they have perceived in their loved one.

One participant's husband did a Quest after she returned from her Quest.

Shortly after returning from my Vision Quest in the United States, my husband took off to the mountains just north of Cape Town to do a four-day Vision Quest. Upon his return home I was mesmerised by the life and passion in his eyes. I know what you must see, Denise, when we all return from our circles! It's been easy and natural talking to him, now, about all aspects of this side of my life.

Another participant wrote about the transition that she experienced on her return.

I came back home, unable to give words to what I had experienced. I felt free and I felt a need to protect that freedom. Fitting into the rhythm of my family environment posed a new challenge. My husband and I could not connect. Yet my whole being cried out for connection. The yin and yang parts of myself had some hard work to find wholeness. The Vision Quest was truly a search for my own identity and re-evaluating my life. It was a big adventure and it put me back feeling in control of my life. Now I feel more control over the choices I make.

This participant and her husband were able to overcome, in a positive way, the temporary distance they experienced after her return from the Quest, but their experience was not uncommon. Be aware that some people in your life may feel unsettled if you are changed by your experience.

Another Quest participant had consistently taken the role of a helper/caretaker for everyone in her life. After the Quest she felt a surge of empowerment and self-assertiveness fill her and she decided to make some changes in her life. This intimidated others who had entered into the victim/saviour relationship dynamic with her. She said some friends were upset with her. 'What do you mean you are not going to be in charge of the car pool any more?', 'What do you mean you are not going to watch my kids every Friday night?' However, she said that extraordinary strength came from finding her truth and listening to her inner voice. It took a few months for friends to adjust to the 'new' person. Although a few friends fell away, this participant reported that she felt a much deeper connection to people because her friendships were based on mutual respect and not need.

Even if you don't have the support of other people, there is power in following the guidance that occurs during your Quest. If you are concerned about the changes that a Quest might bring into your relationships ask yourself, 'Do I want to live a life fulfilling the expectations of other people or do I want to be an individual who is willing to make a stand in life? Do I want to be a person who lives their truth? Do I want to be a person who says, "This is what I believe. This is who I am. This is my path."?' If you are, then the changes that occur in your relationships will be for the good of all.

A Quest can change the way you view the world. There are two ways of looking at the world. One is the ordinary way that people born into Western culture have come to accept. Ordinary reality dictates that objects and events in life, though they may seem to influence each other, are nevertheless separate. A second way of observing the world is that there is a sacred pattern of energy that underlies all life and that, in the most profound sense, we are not separate from the world around us.

We are trained from early childhood in Western culture to embrace the first way of being. Even though in school sports, for example, we are taught about team spirit and working together. However, a deeper perception reveals an energy of competitiveness that underlies our entire educational system. Believing in a random and separate world has survival value. In desperate times isolation, competitiveness and separation perhaps can keep one alive. After a Quest, however, a belief in a flowing universe often evolves, where every act has ramifications on the world at large. This brings a quality of mystery and insight that greatly enriches life but can at the same time bring concern and puzzlement from friends and family. 'What do you mean that the wind told you to quit your job. Are you crazy?'

One participant wrote about how the shift of perception of reality affected his life.

For me the Vision Quest offered a significant shift in how I perceive reality. Before the Quest I perceived reality much the same as a photograph of a moment in time. Now reality seems more like a hologram of the same. I'm able to allow other

perspectives to be experienced as my life unfolds. My Vision
Quest has been a joyous journey, opening my heart and mind
to the beautiful depths of feelings. It truly empowers me to be of
service to others in this life.

After a Quest, individuals often report changes in their
decision-making process. They report feeling a greater sense
of certainty once they have made a decision; and they find
the amount of time needed to make a decision is shorter.

In the usual course of life, to make a decision we embark
on a logical course of investigation. We gather and compare the facts and then, through a process of elimination
and analysis, we come to a conclusion. However, there is
another way to make decisions. During your Quest, when
you begin to step into that quiet inner place of wisdom and
clarity it sets in motion a new way of making decisions.
Instead of the linear process, you may find that you 'just
know' the right choice. Sometimes there won't be any con-
crete data to prove your decision, but there is a gut
response inside you that says, 'This just feels right.' In my
experience, decisions made in this fashion are often much
more satisfying, for they have emerged through intuition
and instinct. It *is* valuable to gather and analyse data for any
life-affecting decision, but making a decision solely on logic
and rational reasoning often yields less beneficial results
than a choice made, after amassing information, from
intuition.

There is often but a moment to make a choice, and in the past
I usually let the moment pass and later regretted for a long

time my decisions reached through inaction. Now I find that I am able to make decisions much more easily and effortlessly.

R.M.

Yes, something happened to me on Sacred Island. I don't know if it's so important to analyse what happened because I have lived my whole life analysing everything. After the Vision Quest I decided to give up analysing so much and to give room for more miracles in my life.

M.J.

Problems don't necessarily disappear after your Quest, but often you experience a shift in the way you view them. Instead of seeing problems as insurmountable difficulties they become challenges; personal obstacles are seen in the context of growth and spiritual development.

Before Joseph came to the Vision Quest, he had had a boundary dispute for eleven years with his next-door neighbour. During those years his neighbour could be downright nasty to Joseph and his wife, making neighbourhood life sometimes intolerable. After the Quest, Joseph went out to his garden, looked over the fence and saw his neighbour in his garden. It was the first time in almost eleven years that Joseph didn't feel a tightness in the pit of his stomach when he saw him. He surprised himself by saying 'Hi!' to his neighbour. The neighbour was just as surprised as Joseph was by this friendly gesture. Although the border dispute didn't go away, it bothered Joseph less and less. He said that after the Quest he began to see all the value that he had gained over the eleven years' disagreement and it completely altered the way he viewed his relationship with his neighbour.

Sometimes life is like a still pool that looks clear for the top few inches, but beneath the clear water there lies a deep reservoir of silt and algae. If a fresh, crystal-clear stream flows into the stagnant pool it stirs up the pool so it looks murky. Eventually, however, the pool becomes clear to the golden sandy bottom. This can parallel what can occur during and after a Quest. Sometimes, before the Quest, life may seem calm and serene but beneath the surface are a number of unresolved issues. The Vision Quest is like the clear water flowing into a stagnant pool stirring up old issues. So it may seem that after the Quest there is a surfeit of problems. These difficulties may be uncomfortable but it is healthy to deal with them and eventually they vanish from your life.

Going on a Vision Quest doesn't necessarily mean that you won't have any problems afterwards. But what often occurs is that your ability to deal with problems becomes quicker, so that you don't hold on to them for so long. Even though most people think they don't want problems, problems aren't really the dilemma: it is *attachment* to problems that creates difficulty. For example, if everyone's problems were thrown into a circle and you could choose any, wouldn't you be quick to retrieve your own? Part of the experience of living on the planet is having problems, and your ability to detach from them can free up life-force energy so you become more vital and exuberant.

It is not uncommon for one's definition of self to alter after a Quest. Often our sense of self comes from definitions that others have given us about who we are. When you take time to be quiet and sit in nature, the boundaries of self expand beyond the body. The limitations imposed by others and society begin to lift so you see yourself in a new light.

During the Quest I felt layers of my inner being were being peeled away like an onion. As one layer was exposed and cleaned, there would be another. I worked through deep childhood traumas that I had never been aware were affecting me, leading me to a peace and connectedness that I had never felt before. Looking back, the difference I feel is that of a parachute full of old stuff being dragged around behind me being released, leaving me feeling much lighter, almost floating.

Wild Flower, a New Zealand international flight attendant.

People often report that before the Quest self-esteem comes from what they do; afterwards it begins to come from who they are.

When I decided to go to the Vision Quest I really didn't have any good reasons for travelling to the other side of the world. Maybe I had to get far enough away from my normal environment, and go to a safe place where I couldn't run away from myself and my life any more. Before the Quest I was a doer. I gained acceptance in life through what I did. Also I had difficulties with my emotions. I never met a person who I trusted enough to tell about my feelings. I felt that I was covered by thick ice. Living was like driving a car with ten safety belts on. Life was a 'slow' depression that caused different pains to my body. As a result of the Quest I have learned to feel more and this has been the beginning of my new life. I still have problems with things like letting go. But now I have insight about it and I believe that I can learn more. I am at the beginning and I won't stop.

Mervi, chiropodist, Finland

In normal life we usually identify ourselves in the context of our family, which is usually defined as relatives and close friends. Often after a Quest the sense of self expands beyond ordinary parameters to include a greater circle of relationship and family.

I left the Vision Quest with such happiness and confidence; something I have always been lacking. The whole concept of family now has a different meaning. Family is now, to me, everything in the universe.

Lin B., British occupational reflexologist

I have been particularly encouraged to see the vast array of newly discovered talents and abilities that emerge for so many after a Quest. Lin B. also mentioned that she was now able to see her own previously undiscovered abilities.

As I looked back on my life I realised I always had the strength to get through difficult situations and was able to see the healing power that I always had. I now have the courage to help people with this same power.

Quests, no matter what form they take, contribute to the understanding that there are no accidents in life. Even mundane aspects of life are propelling you on your spiritual path. Even those things which you judged in yourself or in others are 'on purpose'. Every experience you have is allowing you to become brighter, lighter and closer to the Creator. There is a divine plan for your life and everything that happens to you is a part of that plan. This can bring a deep sense of relief, for many people feel a longing for purpose in life. The power of the Quest is to allow you to understand the deep current of intent that propels your life and at the same time recognises that you are doing exactly what you should be doing in life. Every experience has brought you to where you are now; and where you are now is at a pinnacle in your evolution. *Even if you don't leave a Quest knowing exactly what your purpose is, you are nevertheless fulfilling your purpose perfectly. You always have been.*

Impatience and lack of acceptance usually have at their root a lack of self-esteem. For as self-esteem grows, an acceptance of life circumstances grows. It is not uncommon, after a Quest, to have a deeper sense of patience for self and others. The impatient desire to achieve more and faster is often replaced with a calmer motivation, which usually produces greater results with less effort. Susan, a systems analyst from Chicago said:

In the four years since my Quest, I feel much more satisfied with what I have and who I am. This doesn't mean that I don't have goals. I do have goals and things I want to attain in my life. I used to feel that if I wasn't constantly achieving,

I wasn't a worthwhile person. However, now I strive for goals because it's fun, rather than feeling a compulsion to be a high achiever.

Lennart is a very respected, high-level Swedish business-man. He wrote to me describing how he felt he gained more patience and acceptance after his Quest on Sacred Island.

I am really much more happy with my life after the Vision Quest. In my daily life, now there have been not only one, but many occasions when I have been surprised about the way I have managed to handle things. My employees have mentioned more than once that they have a leader and coach who has high human values. I realised very strongly during the Vision Quest course that I often judge people. I want them to behave like me, for example, to be on time for the class, and not ask silly questions etc. I noticed your patience; how you accepted people, even if they were late and how you answered every question, and even if it was quite clear that the person who asked the question just wanted to hear her/his own voice. I had an instantaneous shift, which I experienced during the course.

Another very noticeable shift, which has occurred and grown stronger each day, is that I have stopped trying so hard to achieve my goals. I have become much more subtle [relaxed] in my approach to daily tasks and I dare say that I am more successful that way. When I look back on my life and think about how many times I have failed because of trying too hard, it is a relief finally to become 'enlightened' and realise that 'it's not good, it's not bad, we have not seen the whole story yet.' My stress level is lower, not because I have less to do in my work, but because something has changed in me and I now see things differently.

I am more content with my life. At the Quest I was looking for guidance about how I should continue my life. I was very uncomfortable and unsure about my daily life. However, during my time on the island, I realised that I am on the right path. There is a purpose in my present job and as soon as I have completed that purpose I will be able to continue. This I have felt strongly [since the Quest]. I also dare say that I enjoy the present moment in a completely new way.

Lennart also mentioned that he realised that the focus of his Quest wasn't to overcome fears, it was to learn to live at peace in the present.

Quite early I realised that the Quest wasn't for me to meet my fears but more to understand that this is it . . . I live here and now. This has made me feel much more secure in my life. [Because I am a man who is always busy], it was a relief when, during the second day [of my Quest], I realised that I was content and felt inspiration flow through my body . . . without doing anything. For me, with all my demands always to do something, this was a relief. This is probably the most important thing I learned during the Vision Quest. I have definitely incorporated this into the way I live and work today and I don't feel frustrated when I don't manage to fulfil all my plans. I know there is a new day tomorrow.

It is difficult to live fully if you are afraid of dying. Fear of death can be a sinister subconscious undercurrent in your life. When you begin to see yourself and your life in a larger context during your Quest, there emerges a sense of self that is beyond the body. You realise that you inhabit a body, but you are not your body. You are Spirit, infinite and ever-lasting. When this realisation occurs, fear of death begins to drop away and a deep relaxation fills its place.

One participant spoke about how her Quest changed her perception of death.

Many things have changed since the Quest. For example, I'm not afraid of death any more. In addition, different fears have begun to drop away. For example, the first time that I ever really enjoyed flying was my journey from Seattle to New York [after the Quest]. It was wonderful! I was sitting on the plane, drum in my arms, having fun. The whole experience on the island was the best time of my life!

Post Vision Quest Suggestions

1. Be understanding of the response of others to your Quest

It's important when you return home after a Quest to be sensitive to the responses of others. You may feel like a hero returning from a great odyssey and, instead of a hero's welcome, you are met with indifference, disbelief, envy or even hostility. It's important to be compassionate, as it can be difficult for others to understand what you have been through unless they have been through a similar experience. Once, immediately following a very intensive inner Quest in Europe, I went to visit a friend who had a large house in

London. I arrived at her home feeling such a deep sense of overwhelming compassion and love for all living beings that when the housekeeper opened the door, I embraced him and told him I loved him. Though secretly I'm sure he was very pleased, on the surface he was quite startled by my unexpected sentiments. This experience deepened my realisation that it's not only valuable to take time to become grounded after a Quest but it's also important to be understanding of the responses of others.

Sometimes there is an advantage in not talking at length about your experience in the weeks and months afterwards. It is a seed within you that has been planted in your deep consciousness that will sprout and bear fruit in the years to come. And like all seeds in their initial stages of growth, it needs to be protected. Those who want to know will seek you out. Sometimes talking too much about your experience to those who don't understand can diminish the sacredness of your vision; so be discriminate about what you say and to whom you say it.

2. Be wary of high expectations

High expectations can sometimes be a difficulty after a Quest. Tony's marriage was falling apart and he thought that if he did a Quest it would help keep his marriage together. He was disappointed to find after his Quest that his wife still wanted to leave him. He did report, however, that he felt that his Quest helped him deal with the separation in a more harmonious way. Sometimes high expectations come from family and friends who expect dramatic changes in their loved one; this occurs especially with teenage Quests. A Quest is very individual. Sometimes people have immediate and dramatic results. Sometimes the results from a Quest are deep and internal without exterior results for months or years. Honour the process in whatever form it takes.

3. Don't make sudden changes

Sometimes immediately after a Quest there is such a sense of exhilaration and freedom that there is a tendency to want to throw off the fetters of society and make immediate and dramatic changes in life. This course of action has served some people who otherwise might have become bogged down in old patterns and habits; however, for most people I suggest letting some time go by while your vision becomes integrated into your everyday life. Don't make any dramatic changes until you have had some time to assess their implications in your life.

Integrating your Vision into your Life

When you return to ordinary life the dishes still need to be washed, laundry needs to be done, and bills need to be paid. In Zen Buddhism there is a maxim, 'Before enlightenment, chop wood and carry water . . . after enlightenment, chop wood and carry water.' The Quest is not about turning away from ordinary life but rather embracing it with compassion, integrity and joy. Though the outward form of life may remain the same, your inner life begins to change. It's as if an ember of spirit in the soul has been fanned by the winds of heaven to become an inner flame that will burn deeply and brightly throughout life.

A Quest done with intent and open heart is like a pebble dropped in a still pool whose ripples will touch the farthest shores of your consciousness. Even in those times, after a Quest, when the vision seems so far away – 'Was it all a dream? Did it really happen?' – the inner flame continues to burn. Your vision will grow inside you. Even in the darkest moments. Even when you are unsure of yourself. Even when you are angry or afraid. This is the power of the vision.

May your Quest be the beginning of an adventure that leads you to the centre of the soul.

Notes

Chapter 1

1 Fire/Lame Deer, John and Erdoes, Richard, *Lame Deer: Seeker of Visions*, Pocket Books, New York, 1976, pp. 1–6/Davis-Poynter, London, 1973.

Chapter 2

1 Campbell, Joseph, *Hero with a Thousand Faces*, Princeton University Press, Princeton, 1970/Grafton Books, London, 1988.

2 See Linn, Denise, *Sacred Space, Clearing and Enhancing the Energy of Your Home*, Rider Books, London, 1995.

3 For further study of signs see Linn, Denise, *Signposts*, Rider Books, London, 1996.

Chapter 3

1 Mai-Mai Sze, *The Way of Chinese Painting*, Random House, New York, 1959.

Chapter 5

1 Brown, Joseph Epes, *The Sacred Pipe, Black Elk's Account of Seven Rites of the Oglada Sioux*, University of Oklahoma Press, 1953.

Further Information

Denise offers professional certification training programmes in Interior Alignment© as well as seminars and workshops on other subjects, including her annual Vision Quest.

For information about her seminars in the Northern Hemisphere contact:
New Life Promotions
Arnica House, 170 Campden Hill Road, London W8 7AS, UK Tel: 44-171-938 3788

In the Southern Hemisphere contact:
New Life Promotions
Locked Bag 19, Pyrmont, NSW 2009, Australia
Tel: 61-2-9552-6833

Vision Quest Seminars in the United States contact:
Denise Linn Seminars
PO Box 75657, Seattle, Washington 98125-065, USA

Vision Quest Seminars in Canada contact:
Pathwork
Jy and Gail Chiperzak
RR2, Marmora, Ontario, KOK 2MO, Canada
Tel: 1-613-472-1217

For Vision Quest Seminars in Europe contact:
Ellie Baker
20 Laurier Road, London NW5 1SG, UK
Tel: 44-171-267-6873

For Vision Quest Seminars in Africa contact:
Lynette and Brian Orman
PO Box 245, Noordhoek 7985, South Africa
Tel: 27-21-789-1833

For Vision Quest Seminars in Australia contact:
Native Journeys
110 Auburn Road, Hawthorne, Melbourne, Victoria 3122,
Australia Tel: 61-3-818-8810

For Vision Quest facilitator training contact:
The School of Lost Borders
Box 55, Big Dine, California, 93513, USA

For information about Denise's audio tapes contact:
QED Recording Services
Lancaster Road, New Barnet, Hertfordshire EN4 8AS, UK
Tel: 44-181-441-7722

For a Sacred Space Products catalogue:
PO Box 75036, Seattle, Washington 98125-0036, USA

Index